D1368128

MORE LEARNING
IN LESS TIME

*Some books are to be tasted,
others to be swallowed, and some
few to be chewed and digested.*

Sir Francis Bacon

MORE LEARNING IN LESS TIME

A Guide for Students and Professionals

THIRD EDITION

Norma B. Kahn

College of Arts and Sciences
University of Pennsylvania

TEN SPEED PRESS
Berkeley, California

1☉
TEN SPEED PRESS
P.O. Box 7123
Berkeley, CA 94707

Cover design by Fifth Street Design
Text design by Sarah Levin
Type set by Wilsted & Taylor

Library of Congress Cataloging-in-Publication Data:
Kahn, Norma B.
    More learning in less time: a guide for students and
        professionals / Norma B. Kahn.—3rd ed.
    Bibliography: p. 2
    ISBN 0-89815-321-2
    1. Study, Method of.   I. Title.
    LB2395.K27   1989
    378.1'7'0281—dc20   89-4633   CIP

Printed in the United States of America

1   2   3   4   5—93   92   91   90   89

■ Preface

More Learning in Less Time has evolved in four versions, over a period of twenty years. Each version was revised as students and teachers responded to it. The first version was a mimeographed collection of materials called "Efficient and Effective Study." The second version, now called *More Learning in Less Time*, was published by Hayden Book Co., with the knowledgeable and genial guidance of editor Robert Boynton. The next version was the revised edition, in 1984, with the continued editorial encouragement of Bob Boynton, who by this time had formed Boynton/Cook Company, extraordinary publishers of textbooks related primarily to English education.

I am grateful to George Young of Ten Speed Press for giving me the opportunity to update and expand *More Learning in Less Time* in this third edition. While keeping the book relatively brief, I have reorganized and expanded several sections and improved many of the recommendations, and added several new sections. The new sections are "Studying Math and Technical Subjects," "Learning a Foreign Language," "Keeping Up in Your Profession: Lifelong Learning," and the appendix, "Copyright Law: An Increasing Concern to Students and Professionals." Finally, the bibliographies have been updated, and some illustrations have been inserted to lighten the prose and the reader's day.

The two earlier editions were developed with the help of my colleagues and students at the University of Pennsylvania in the Graduate School of Education, when I taught in and directed the Reading and Language Arts Program, administered programs in writing and literature, and supervised the University Reading/Study Improvement Service. I am indebted especially to Dr. Susan L. Lytle for reading closely drafts of the first two editions and also for introducting me to Isaac Watts' *Improvement of the Mind* (1741). In 1983, I found a 1787 edition of Watts' book and realized that quoting from it, in *More Learning and Less Time*, would reinforce my own statements in more elegant and venerable language and would also add an interesting historical dimension.*

Sections of this third edition have benefited from recommendations by two of my previous colleagues in the Graduate School of Education, Dr. Carol S. Brown and Myrna L. Cohen, and by several of my present colleagues in the College of Arts and Science, Assistant Deans Flora Cornfield, Augusto Hacthoun, and Eric Schneider, and Vice Dean for Language Instruction Barbara Freed.

For advice about studying in various disciplines, I am indebted to the following professors: at the University of Pennsylvania, Drs. Jonathan Baron (Psychology), Michael Katz (History), Richard D. Paul (Computer and Information Science), David Shale (Mathematics), and Paul Soven (Physics); and at Bard College, Dr. Mark Lytle (History). For the section on studying law, I was advised by Professor Louis B. Schwartz, formerly of the University of Pennsylvania Law School, now of the University of California's Hastings School of the Law, and also by attorneys Arthur Berger and Marilyn T. Benjamin. Arthur Seidel, Esq., has counseled me generously on copyright law. The section on library research was reviewed by John Kupersmith, formerly reference librarian at the University of Pennsylvania, now Assistant Director of Computer-Based Information Services at the University of Texas at Austin.

My husband, Alan Kahn, helped me compose my first drafts of the section on studying law. Our children, Emily Kahn, James Thurman Kahn, and Marcia Kahn Kaminker, and our sons-in-law, Martin Kaminker and Noah Freedman, recommended ways to make various sections of each

---

* Watts' book was based in part on John Locke's *An Essay Concerning Human Understanding*, which was written in 1690 and was among the most widely read and influential books of the eighteenth century. Watts himself was a great English clergyman and the author of many hymns still sung today, including "O God, Our Help in Ages Past" and "Joy to the World."

edition clearer and stronger. I thank them with love and pride that grows with each year.

Ann Bailey, Linda Skinner, and Lenore Wilkas have helped me prepare my manuscript for publication under a close deadline. I am grateful for their thorough and dependable assistance.

I added the new section on lifelong learning when my own convictions were further encouraged by several paragraphs in Cyril O. Houle's *Continuing Learning in the Professions* (San Francisco: Jossey-Bass Publishers, 1980):

"A profession has the collective responsibility to honor and foster . . . zest for learning in all its members. . . . It has a similar obligation to help its members develop the ability to learn how to learn. . . .

"Every person who practices a profession needs . . . to be aware of relevant new developments in its basic disciplines, to improve competence . . . and to preserve an appropriate perspective on worklife and not be engulfed by it . . ." (pp. 306–307).

Dr. Houle affirms that the best way to maintain zest for learning and to prevent boredom or burnout in one's profession is to maintain other intellectual interests throughout adult life. Then "more than a few practitioners will make the personal discovery that what they learn outside their profession gives them valuable new insights into the work they do," and "later in life, when professional practice usually diminishes and finally ceases, the zest for experience will continue and an independent dignity and resourcefulness remain" (pp. 48–49).

I hope that *More Learning in Less Time* will enhance the education and accomplishment of students and continual learners of all ages.

■ Acknowledgments

The author and publishers wish to thank the following who have kindly given permission for the use of copyright material:

Graduate Record Examination Board, Educational Testing Service, for four items from the 1988–1989 GRE Information Bulletin.

Heinemann Boynton/Cook Publishers and Sandra Boynton for Sandra Boynton's illustration of the quotation from Francis Bacon's "Of Studies."

Harry G. Henn and Practising Law Institute, for excerpts from Mr. Henn's book, *Copyright Law: A Practitioner's Guide*, 2nd ed., 1988 (supp. 1989).

Jossey-Bass Publishers, San Francisco, CA, for quotations from *Continuing Learning in the Professions* by Cyril O. Houle, 1980.

Leonard Miller, for his questionnaire about test anxiety, Copyright © 1979.

Viking Penguin, a division of Penguin Books USA, Inc., for the graphic representation of Abraham Maslow's Hierarchy of Needs, from *The Third Force: The Psychology of Abraham Maslow*, by Frank Goble, which was published by Pocket Books in 1971, by arrangement with Grossman Publishers, Inc. Copyright © 1970 by Thomas Jefferson Research Center.

Every effort has been made to trace all the copyright holders, but if any have been overlooked the publishers will be pleased to make the necessary arrangement.

■ Contents

■ Introduction

This is a "ways-to" book, not a "how-to" one. It invites you to try various ways to learn more in less time, and to adapt them according to your individual style and purposes. The book is organized and formatted to help you understand it more quickly and remember it more readily as you try the ways recommended. Many sections are segmented and indented beyond usual paragraphing, to make the content that much clearer.

You are likely to learn more from this book, in less time, if you start by looking through the table of contents and marking the sections that most appeal to you and if you try the self-evaluation described below before reading any other part of the book thoroughly.

Then, start reading one of the sections that especially interests you. You might want to continue reading in the order of your interest, or you might want to read from beginning to end. Whatever order you choose, use a quick marking method in the table of contents and in the margins of the sections; for example, use checks to remind yourself of which sections you read and found interesting and arrows to remind yourself of which sections or ideas you want to try applying. (See pp. 101–102 for more detailed suggestions for marking tables of contents, to make them records of your reading and guides to action.)

If you are concerned about studying a subject not discussed directly in this book, look for sections that seem applicable for your purposes. For example, to study pharmacology, read the section on "Remembering Effectively" and consider how you could apply the principles to the material you have to learn.

■ Self-Evaluation

■ Checklist of factors involved in reading, writing, and study

The checklist on page two can help you evaluate your strengths and weaknesses in reading, writing, and study:

1. In the columns on the right, check the factors that seem to you areas of need or concern.
2. In the column on the left, check the factors that seem to you areas of strength.
3. Leave the line blank next to any factor that is neither a strength nor a need or concern for you.
4. Add any additional factors that seem significant to you as strengths or needs or concerns.

■ Using the checklist

If most of the needs or concerns that you checked have to do with problems in reading and study skills (the upper half of the checklist) and most of your strengths are attitudes (the lower half), this guidebook is likely to be all that you need in order to read, write, and study more effectively and efficiently.

If you have checked both skills and attitudes as needs or

CHECKLIST

DATE OF
FIRST CHECK _____   DATE OF
RECHECK _____   YEAR OF LAST
VISION TEST _____

Area of strength	Factors in reading, writing, study	Need or concern:	
		major	minor
	Comprehending written material		
	Responding critically and creatively		
	Retaining information		
	Taking notes from reading		
	Taking notes from listening		
	Time management		
	Vocabulary		
	Pronouncing unfamiliar words		
	Taking examinations		
	Writing papers		
	Rate of reading		
	Self-image as a reader		
	Self-image as a writer		
	Tension when reading		
	Preparation in previous school(s)		
	Present curriculum		
	Present instruction		
	Support/pressures from home		
	Coping with present environment		
	Attitude toward reading		
	Attitude toward writing		
	Concentration		
	Self-confidence		
	Will power		
	Motivation		
	Procrastination		
	Certainty/uncertainty about goals		

concerns (especially the attitudinal factors of poor concentration and lack of will power and motivation), you are likely to need more than this guide in order to improve.

You might best avail yourself of some combination of the aids provided by a university reading/writing improvement service or learning center. These services are likely to include the following:

1. Interviews to help students evaluate their strengths and needs in reading, writing, and study
2. Reading/writing/study improvement courses
3. Individual tutoring
4. Instructional materials designed to be used independently
5. Workshops on overcoming test anxiety
6. Referral for personal and/or career counseling
7. Referral for tutoring in oral or written expression

When you have incorporated many of the procedures recommended in this book into your reading and study habits, recheck the checklist. Use a different color pen or a different symbol so that you can easily compare your present self-evaluation with your earlier one.

If your present self-evaluation indicates that attitudinal factors still contribute to your reading or study problems, consultation with a counseling psychologist is probably desirable. If your self-evaluation indicates that skill factors still contribute to your reading or study problems, consultation with a reading/writing/study specialist at the university learning center should be helpful.

If you have strong fears of examinations and aren't sure whether you should consult a professional about them, use the following "Self-Evaluation Regarding Test-Anxiety," developed by Dr. Leonard Miller, who is Associate Director and Chief Psychologist at the University of Pennsylvania Counseling Service.

■ Self-evaluation regarding test-anxiety*

There are many reasons that account for students not doing well on examinations: for example, being unprepared, feeling ill, missing an important lecture or assignment, construction noise outside the window, and so forth. Some students do not do well on examinations because they become overly tense and "test-anxious."

If you answer "yes" to many of the following questions, you may have "test-anxiety." If so, you should seek help from a mental health professional who is trained to help people deal with anxiety.

1. Do you block or freeze when studying for an exam?
2. Do you go blank during exams?
3. Do you frequently forget information that you previously learned?
4. Do you find the words meaningless as you read test questions?
5. Do you need to reread test questions in order to comprehend them?
6. Do you find yourself plotting ways to escape from a test (sneaking out, feigning illness)?
7. Do you—before, during, after exams—have physical symptoms such as rapid heart rate, excessive perspiration, tense muscles, queasy stomach, nausea?
8. Do you have difficulty maintaining concentration while studying or taking exams?
9. Do you panic as time runs out during an exam?
10. Do you worry about how you are doing on an exam compared to others taking the exam?
11. Do you worry about failing an exam?
12. Do you find yourself wishing you were out of school, working—especially just before exams?
13. Do you panic on a test if you don't know the answer to a question?
14. Do you get distracted easily while taking an exam?
15. Do you find that you get so tired from worrying about exams that you almost don't care how well you do by the time the test comes?

■ Organizing Work and Budgeting Time

Organizing work and budgeting time are essential to effective and efficient reading and study. To take these essential steps, you will need a calendar-memorandum book. If you don't own such a book, or at least a calendar with large blocks for each date, buy one or the other as soon as possible.

Specific suggestions about organizing work and budgeting time are included with almost every kind of reading, writing and study described in this guide.

Two general recommendations should be helpful at this point:

1. Keep in mind the useful concepts of "chunking" and "clustering":

     Chunking, as used here, means identifying the parts or subgroups of extended materials or tasks, in order to accomplish more readily and effectively what you need to do. Chunking can help prevent procrastination and improve concentration and memory.

     Chunking when you read and study is like chunking when you eat. When you eat meat, you chunk by cutting up the meat, then you chew and swallow one bite at a time; when you eat peas, you cluster peas on your fork, then you chew and swallow the group all together.

     Similarly, when you read and study you should chunk and cluster: cut pieces too large for one bite and group small items for one bite. To digest a textbook chapter, don't read the chapter from beginning to end.

Instead, chunk the chapter by sections. (See the pages on "Mastering Textbook Material" and "Studying Math and Technical Subjects" for steps to try after chunking.)

To prepare for an exam, gain an overall view of the total material to be covered, perhaps by making a table of contents for your class notes and reading the summaries of all chapters in a comprehensive book on the subject. Then chunk the material and study one chunk at a time.

> When you read and study you should "chunk" and "cluster": CUT UP pieces too large for one bite and GROUP small items for one bite.

When you have to learn many details, like new words in a foreign language or scientific terms, cluster by grouping about five words that are related in some way; then study the words one cluster or group at a time. Fit such brief-task study into brief periods of time, like when you are waiting for a train.

You can apply the idea of chunking to many tasks you find difficult to begin or to complete, like packing for a long trip; organizing stacks of many kinds of material that you've accumulated in a spare room; filing hundreds of articles you've clipped from magazines and newspapers; or planning your sabbatical or retirement.

The notion of chunking is useful in simply noting what you have to do each day. For instance, you can write "Call," "See," "Do" at intervals down a memo page and jot down your notes under the appropriate category. Similarly, on separate pages, you can write at the top, in order, the next two months and the next three seasons. (I group these pages in my small loose-leaf memo book behind an alphabetic divider labeled E for "Eventually.") Whenever you think of something you should do within these periods, write it on the appropriate page. When the time comes to note what you have to do for each day, retrieve your earlier ideas by consulting your lists for the months or seasons.

2. As you look over your plans for a particularly crowded day, weekend, or vacation-with-work, note next to each task the approximate amount of time the task is likely to take; then add up the time periods you've noted and consider the result. You are likely to feel amazed and relieved that the many separate tasks that seemed so burdensome will fit into the time available; and so you can work more effectively and efficiently— and also look forward to the recreation you'll have time for, after all. Sometimes, however, you may find that the tasks do not fit into the time available; therefore, some of them will have to be postponed until a different day, weekend, or vacation-with-work. If you will note in your memorandum book when you plan to accomplish the tasks that must be postponed, you are likely to concentrate better on the work at hand.

∎ Remembering Effectively

The following information about remembering supports many of the suggestions in this guide.* If as you read this book you wonder why a particular suggestion is made, you will probably find the reasons among these "principles of remembering."

To remember details, you should:

1. Care about, or be genuinely interested in, remembering the information.
2. Give full attention to what is to be remembered.
3. Impress the information upon your mind clearly and correctly the first time you encounter it.
4. Associate what you want to learn with other related information.
5. Think of details to be learned in terms of a related structure, or create a visually memorable structure for them.
6. If there are more than about five details, group them in appropriate clusters.
7 Process the information by using several senses while thinking about the information (for example, recite aloud what you recall from the material read, and check for accuracy; write briefly what you recall, and check for accuracy; discuss what you are learning with others).
8. Think, "I *will* remember" (an intent to remember is essential to effective remembering)

---

* The information is derived from two valuable sources: Donald A. Norman's *Memory and Attention* (New York: Wiley, 1976) and James Weinland's *How to Improve Your Memory* (New York· Harper and Row, 1986)

9. Review the information within twenty-four hours, preferably before sleep.

> Think of details to be
> learned in terms of a
> related structure or create
> a visually memorable
> structure for them.

To remember extended reading material, you should also:

1. Impress upon your memory the *internal* organization of the new material before reading the material further.
2. Connect the information with related *external* information.
3. Chunk the material into units that are appropriate to its organization and contain no more than four to seven items.
4. Process the material chunk by chunk (in effect, chew and swallow each chunk before biting off another chunk).

Note: If there is something you want to *forget*, avoid as many of the above steps as possible.

■ Improving Listening and Notetaking from Listening

Listening, like reading, should be active; it should involve constant thinking, making connections, evaluating. Notetaking from listening, like notetaking from reading, should include not only what the speaker or writer said, but also critical response to what was said or written. In short, you need to *make* notes as well as *take* notes.

> Listening, like reading, should be active. . . . you need to MAKE notes as well as TAKE notes.

1. Prepare for listening and learning.
   a) When you know the subject in advance, preview or review related reading in order to recognize and organize main ideas and terms more easily (that is, increase your background in the subject in a way that makes clear its general organization or structure and some key terms).
   b) Use a large loose-leaf notebook for notetaking so that you can rearrange the pages for study purposes, such as comparing, contrasting, and synthesizing.
2. Create notes that will provide a visually memorable impression of the organization of the material.

a) Write only on the front side of the loose-leaf page so that your writing will show up clearly (no writing will show through from the other side) and so that you can rearrange the material without having to flip over pages.

b) Use deep indentation to impress upon your mind the relationship between supporting ideas and organizing ideas.

> Use deep indentation
> to impress upon your mind
> the relationship between
> supporting ideas and
> organizing ideas.

c) In a class for which notetaking seems especially difficult, leave blank lines at the end of each paragraph or section so that later you can fill in clarifying or supplementary information.

3. Save time by using appropriate abbreviations and symbols.

a) For each course or lecture, decide on abbreviations for words likely to be used frequently. Note your code on the top of the first page on which you use the abbreviation or on a page set aside for the purpose. Three examples of abbreviation are:

p = poetry   rdg = reading
compr'n = comprehension

b) In all courses, also use standard (not personal) symbols. Consult the appendix of a large dictionary for standard symbols. For example:

$\rightarrow$ leads to or results in $\therefore$ therefore
$\leftarrow$ results from $\Rightarrow$ implies
$\equiv$ is defined as $\nRightarrow$ does not imply

c) In scientific courses, buy a dictionary specific to the subject and consult its complete list of standard abbreviations and symbols in the field.

    d) Remember: abbreviations and symbols can save time in writing answers on essay examinations—and they are generally acceptable (1) if they are *standard*, and (2) if, for one or two proper names that will be repeated frequently, you indicate a code on the top of the page (for example, T=Tchaikovsky).

4. During (and after) listening, note on a separate page your own ideas in response to what you have heard.

    a) Noting your own ideas and questions can prevent your speaking out in class prematurely and can enhance your clarity and fluency in speaking when and if you decide to do so.

    b) Your personal notes can be helpful also in guiding your future reading and in providing a source of ideas or questions for research papers and exam answers.

Review your notes within 24 hours.

    c) Include notes about the instructor's approach to—or method of thinking about—the subject, and try to apply a similar approach or method.

5. Review your notes within twenty-four hours, preferably within a half hour.

a) As soon as possible after listening, read over your notes; make corrections where necessary; add clarifying notes on the lines left blank; and note personal comments and questions on a separate page.
b) Underline organizing ideas and key terms with a colored pen or pencil (a small ruler can speed up this process).
c) Recite aloud, from memory, the ideas you have reviewed.
   1) Recite after reviewing each "chunk" of four to seven subpoints about one organizing idea.
   2) At the end, recite the organizing ideas for four to seven chunks.

The learner . . . should always recollect and review his lectures, read over some other author or authors upon the same subject, confer upon it with his instructor or with his associates, and write down the clearest result of his present thoughts, reasonings, and inquiries, which he may have recourse to hereafter, wither to re-examine them, and to apply them to proper use, or to improve them further to his own advantage.

ISAAC WATTS
The Improvement of the Mind
London (1741)

■ Saving Time in Taking Notes from Reading

To save time in taking notes from library books or other material that you should not mark up, imagine that every page is divided into five horizontal sections invisibly labeled A to E, like this:

On a double-column page, the first column can be imagined as labeled *A to E;* the second, *a to e.*

Using this method, reading for a research paper would go like this:

1. Write on the reverse side of your bibliographical card the page numbers and parts-of-pages (that is, A to E) on which you find promising material. For example, notations for a paper on ideas for a new English curriculum might look like this:

On one side of the card:

> Whitehead, Alfred North. THE AIMS OF ED-
> UCATION AND OTHER ESSAYS. New
> York: The Macmillan Co., 1957.

On the reverse side:

~~2C~~	18C	33BDE
3A	21A	35E
6C-E	27DE	38-39A
7A	28B	~~47E~~
13D, E*	10BE	57A
14E	~~31F~~	

2. After *finishing* a book (or as many books as you want to read before taking notes on the material), return to the pages that you have indicated on the back of each bibliographical card. Type notes on index cards from the material that now seems *essential*. Cross out the page notations that you decide are not useful after all (see examples above).

3. As you read, continually reflect upon what you have read. Make a note of your ideas and feelings about the material. For research papers, make notes on separate cards so that you can organize these with other notes for incorporation in your paper.

   For supplementary reading, make notes on full-size paper, with page references in the margin so that you can include these with your notes from the content when you review for exams.

   See the section on "Improving Thinking" (p. 32) for aids in intensifying your reflection about your reading and in improving the quality of the notes you take on your reflections.

---

*The comma means that some material in the middle of DE should not be noted.

■ Developing Reading Versatility

Listed below are suggestions for developing a habit of approaching reading in ways appropriate for your purposes and for the nature of the material—that is, for developing reading versatility. To increase your interest, concentration, and speed in reading any required material for which you have little or no background, develop background on the subject before the reading: attend a lecture on the subject or preview and selectively read material on the same subject which is easier for you or has more illustrations; or try to have an appropriate firsthand experience related to the subject

■ Reading rapidly for key ideas only

1. Every day practice reading faster than is comfortable for you, using material that you want to read anyway but that you are not required to learn, that you find relatively easy, and that looks highly readable (short lines, clear print).

2. Using the material of your choice, take the following steps for about fifteen minutes every day:

   a) Focus on the title of the article. Quickly review what you already know—and think or feel—about the subject

   b) Preview the material, if it is expository in nature (that is, nonfiction), by reading the last paragraphs, headings, and/or the first sentence in every few paragraphs—any organizational aids that might provide, in effect, a map of the material

c) Tell yourself what you know about the material as a result of the preview.

d) Turn the title into a question, or think of a question of interest to you that is likely to be answered in the material. (In reading an article entitled "New Hope for the Slow Reader," you might ask yourself, "What is the new hope for the slow reader, and is there hope for me?")

e) Read, to answer your question, more rapidly than is really comfortable for you. Concentrate on key ideas, not on your eye movements (your eyes will move faster automatically when you comprehend the content faster).

f) After reading as much as you feel you can in this way (usually after encountering four to seven key ideas), tell yourself what you recall in answer to your question. If you skip this step, you will probably forget what you have read, unless you discuss it with someone that day or have a strong interest in the subject.

g) If you can't remember, your speed may have been too fast; review the material selectively for a fuller answer.

3. Measure your increasing ability to read *appropriate* material rapidly; for example, consider approximately how much more you are able to read within the fifteen-minute practice period from week to week. (Avoid wasting time by counting words per minute.)

*B*ooks of importance of any kind, and especially complete treatises on any subject, should be first read in a more general and cursory manner, to learn a little what the treatise promises, and what you may expect from the writer's manner and skill. And for this end I would advise always that the preface be read, and a survey taken of the table of contents, if there be one, before this first survey of the book. By this means you will not only be better fitted to give the book the first reading, but you will be much assisted in your second perusal of it, which should be done with greater attention and deliberation, and you will learn with more ease and readiness what the author pretends to teach

ISAAC WATTS (1741)

■ Reading expository material for study purposes

Such material includes books and articles listed in bibliographies, *not* major textbooks that should be mastered and *not* imaginative literature.

1. Preview the assignment, including:
   a) the preface and/or table of contents;
   b) the summary and conclusion (this *alone* may be sufficient for the preview);
   c) all headings or the first sentence in each long paragraph (if the summary and conclusions are insufficient).
2. Tell yourself from memory what you have learned from the preview

3. Think about:
   a) the purposes of the instructor in making the assignment;
   b) the apparent purposes of the author;
   c) your additional purposes in reading the material.
4. Formulate and note a few questions related to the purposes you have thought about.
5. Read to answer the questions you have formulated.
6. Pause occasionally to try to answer the questions you have formulated.
7. Take brief "notes" *during* reading:
   a) by bracketing in the margins and/or by *very sparse* underlining (if the book is your own);
   b) by noting pages and parts-of-pages (A, B, C, D, E) from which you may want to take written notes eventually. (See p. 14.)
8. Take more extensive notes *after* reading; include any ideas of your own in response to the material.
   a) For summarizing, take (preferably type) notes from your page notations on full-size paper, with sufficient indentations to indicate relationships between organizing ideas and supporting ideas.
   b) For research papers, take notes from your page notations on 3 × 5 index cards or notepad pages.
9. When your reading and notetaking are complete, reread all your notes, *think* about what you have read, and add more notes on your reflections. (See the section on "Critical and Creative Reading," p. 52.)

... *Mnemon, even from his youth to his old age ... when he came to the end of a section or chapter, he always shut his book, and recollected all the sentiments or expressions he had remarked, so that he could give a tolerable analysis and abstract of every treatise he had read, just after he had finished it. Thence he became so well furnished with a rich variety of knowledge.*

ISAAC WATTS (1741)

■ Mastering textbook material*

Use one or more of these aids according to how difficult the material is for you and how thoroughly you should know it.

Within twenty-four hours *before* a lecture on the subject:

1. Preview the chapter (study its "map").
   a) Ask yourself, "What do I already know about the subject of this chapter?"
   b) Read a portion of the table of contents to see how this chapter is related to the ones preceding and following it.
   c) Read the summary of the chapter (usually to be found near the end or at the beginning). If the summary seems clear and full, skip items (d) and (e) below.
   d) If the summary seems inadequate, read all the headings in the chapter and/or the first sentence in every long paragraph.
   e) Study (learn all you can from) pictures, maps, and other graphic aids.
   f) After each step above, ask yourself, "What do I know about the subject now?" and quickly recite your answer to yourself. Check back for accuracy.

---

*Most of these steps are derived from the procedure originally devised by Francis P. Robinson and described in his book *Effective Study*, Rev. ed. (New York: Harper and Row, 1961).

Within twenty-four hours *after* a lecture on the subject review your notes from the lecture, preferably within a half hour (see "Improving Listening and Notetaking from Listening").

2. Question and read each section of the chapter.

   a) Establish a purpose for reading each section. Either make up a question to keep in mind as you read the section (this can be the heading restated as a question, like "What in heaven's name *are* Double Stars?"), or read a problem at the end of the chapter.

> Establish a PURPOSE
> for reading each section
> of a chapter. . . . Read to
> answer a question or
> solve a problem.

   b) Read to answer the question or to solve the problem. (If the material is very difficult, read the first sentence in every paragraph of the section before reading the section fully.)

3. Recite.

   a) Tell yourself, in your own words and from memory, the answer to the question you kept in mind as you read (plus anything else you remember from the section), or solve the problem.

   b) If you can't remember adequately, skim the section again and recite again.

   c) Continually tell yourself, "I *will* remember."

4. Write.

   a) After reading (and reciting) each section, note the main point (the organizing idea, perhaps just the heading) of the section.

      1) Indent deeply to create a visually memorable outline or "map" of the chapter.

      2) Keep your notes so brief that they fit easily on one page (or one page for every twenty to

twenty-five pages of text); your notes are to serve simply as a cue-sheet to aid your memory.

   3) If the book is your own, underline a *few* words and bracket the most important lines in the section.

b) On another sheet of paper, note any questions that come to your mind about the material or any new insights you may have on this or other related subjects.

Continually tell yourself,
"I WILL remember."

5. Review and reflect. When you have completed the chapter (and the one-page outline), reread the outline, underline the main points, and recite as much as you can from memory. Again, reflect, and add any new ideas to the sheet of paper that is separate from the outline.

To summarize, here is the rack of tools* from which to choose for mastering a textbook chapter. To remember all the steps, use the formula *PQ6R*.

TOOLS	CHECK IF USED
Preview (survey) the whole chapter; recite from memory what you have learned from the preview.	☐
Question (set a purpose: formulate a question or read one problem).	☐
Read one section (chunk) to answer the question or to solve the problem. Bracket main ideas in the margin.	☐
Recite your answer to the question or solve the problem.	☐
Write a line or two toward a one-page outline of the whole chapter.	☐
After finishing the chapter	
Review the one-page outline. Recite it from memory.	☐
Reflect critically and creatively. Write brief notes about your reflections and questions on a page separate from the one-page outline.	☐
Review the one-page outline within twenty-four hours.	☐

---

*Most of these steps are derived from the procedure originally devised by Francis P. Robinson and described in his book *Effective Study*, Rev. ed. (New York: Harper and Row, 1961)

■ Studying math and technical subjects

Studying mathematics and technical subjects such as engineering involves primarily solving problems. How can you learn more in less time in these subjects?

1. Find and impress upon your memory a structured overview of the material that you have to learn.
   a) Before starting work on the first problems in a course, preview and read the introductory or summary chapter of the textbook.
   b) Before reading all subsequent chapters, study the organizational aids in the chapter—the summary, the headings, and the graphic material that can give you a visually memorable "map" of the whole chapter.
2. Study the chapter in appropriate chunks—usually one problem per chunk. Studying a chapter in a math or engineering textbook, after previewing the chapter, would go like this:
   a) Read the first problem, or the first assigned problem, at the end of the section or chapter.
   b) Read the matching section until you think you can work the problem.
   c) Work the problem.
   d) Proceed similarly through the rest of the chapter; read the next assigned problem, read the matching section of the text, and work the problem—so that when you have finished the chapter you have also finished the assigned problems.

   Most textbooks requiring problem solving, especially engineering texts, have many examples of one kind of problem. Solving all of them would be unnecessary and far too time-consuming. If you can easily follow the sample problems within the first section of the chapter, you should not have to work more than one of that kind of problem.
3. Be very organized in laying out the problems you work.
   a) Follow the layout shown in the text's examples.

b) Draw figures and visualize the problem before you work it mathematically. Visualizing the problem is essential to solving it—it helps you understand the problem better and enables you to check one type of reasoning against another. On examinations as well as in regular assignments, solve the problems geometrically as well as mathematically.

> Draw figures and visualize the problem before you work it mathematically.

4. Work with a small group of other students on your homework problems, if your instructor approves. This can give you a vital opportunity to actively use the language of math or the technical field as you discuss how you arrived at your answers to the problems. You should study this way for these reasons:
   a) The more background you have about a subject—background that is appropriately structured—the more readily you can learn, remember, and apply new information about the subject.
   b) To remember extended material, you need to learn it one piece at a time, keeping in mind the pattern into which each piece fits. The best way to learn each piece is to use or apply it in an appropriately structured way.
   c) Discussing problems with other students helps you to learn better in many ways, especially because it involves using several senses while thinking about the subject. It can help you clarify your thinking and increase your motivation to learn and remember.

You will need to cope with other elements of the course than the textbook. In math and technical courses, instructors may not always follow the book exactly; in class, they may spend more time on some areas, leave out other areas, and even add areas not included in the book. Usually, instructors assign homework from the problems at the back of the book—but their exams may include problems that are different from those in the book. Ask your instructor for copies of old exams, or see if they are on file in a learning center. Using the old exams, practice applying what you have learned from class and the homework on problems similar to those that you will face on your next exam.

In studying physics, you should find all but two of the recommendations in this section helpful.

Most of the recommendations in this section hold equally for studying physics. The exceptions, the first of which is crucial, are these:

2b) In physics, identifying which concepts or sections of the textbook are involved in a given problem is the core of the problem. Therefore, chunking in the way described here is much too simplified.

2d) In studying introductory physics texts, which usually have thirty to fifty problems at the end of the chapter, you should do approximately ten problems per chapter, unless more are assigned.

■ Reading fiction or poetry for full effect and meaning

1. Consider—and note in writing—during and after reading fiction or poetry:
   a) the effect of the fiction or poetry on you—emotionally, imaginatively, and intuitively, as well as intellectually;
   b) the scenes, lines, phrases, images, that impressed you most.

> Note the effect that the fiction or poetry has on you.

2. Tentatively and briefly, try to answer the following questions (knowing that you will answer them again when you have studied the work more thoroughly):

a) Considering the novel, short story, or poem as a whole, what do you think it means? In brief, what seem to be its themes? State the themes carefully, avoiding statements that are too narrow or too broad.

b) What view of life, or attitude toward life, does the novel, story, or poem reveal? What is your reaction to this view or attitude?

c) What is the value of the novel, story, or poem for you personally? How has the experience of reading it changed you—your attitudes, your feelings, your thinking?

d) What might be the value of this work of art for others?

3. If you wish or need to understand the fiction or poetry more fully, analyze it in detail. Consider how each element of the work contributes to its total effect and meaning. (A work of art is organic, like a tree or a person; in analyzing it, we need to consider how each element that composes it relates to other elements and to the whole.) For detailed questions that might help you analyze fiction, see the pages immediately following. For taking notes to support your analysis, use the time-saving ABCDE method described previously. For notes that might help you analyze poetry, see page 43. (After analyzing the novel, story, or poem in detail, consider again points 1 and 2.)

4. Consult one of the following sources on the subject:

Barnet, Sylvan. *A Short Guide to Writing About Literature*. 5th ed. Glenview, Ill.: Scott Foresman, 1985.

Boynton, Robert W. and Maynard Mack. *Introduction to the Poem*. 3rd ed. Portsmouth, N.H.: Heinemann Boynton/Cook, 1985.

Scholes, Robert, et al. *Elements of Literature: Poetry, Drama, Essay, Film*. New York: Oxford University Press, 1986

5. In analyzing a work of fiction, consider the following elements:

a) Point of view

1) Is the story told by the author, who knows all? Or through one of the characters? Or through several of the characters? Through their minds, or eyes, or both?

2) Does the narrator seem to be reliable? If not, why not?

3) What does the point of view contribute to the total meaning of the novel?

b) Plot

1) What is the scope of the novel in time?

2) What are the major scenes?

3) Does the action seem to develop because of the nature of the characters? Or through societal forces? Or through fate?

4) What is the shape of the story line? Is it a journey or quest? A fall in morals or in fortune? Or a rise and fall? A meeting or marriage? A growing up through experience? An interweaving of story lines?

5) Does the plot have an underlying pattern?

6) What does the plot contribute to the total meaning of the novel?

c) Characters

1) Are the characters "flat"? (Can they be described fully in a few words? Do they change very little in the novel?) Or are they "round"? (Are many of their qualities revealed? Do they develop during the novel?)

2) Which characters are most memorable to you? Why?

3) How are the characters revealed? By what they say and do? By what the narrator says and thinks? By what other characters say? By what the author says directly to the reader?

4) Do any of the characters contrast with one another in significant ways?

5) What do the characters of this novel contribute to the total meaning of the novel?

d) Setting
1) What is the scope of the novel in space or setting?
2) Does the setting seem important to the characters? To the plot?
3) What does the setting contribute to the total meaning of the novel?
e) Language or diction
1) Is the novel composed largely of conversation? Does the conversation seem true to life?
2) Is the novel simply a reporting of events?
3) Is the novel written with poetic imagery? What are the central images or metaphors?

4) What is the nature of the diction? Is it formal? Informal? Colloquial? Slang? Does it change in the course of the novel?
5) What does the language or diction contribute to the total meaning of the novel?
f) Tone (a quality of style that reveals or creates attitude, like "tone of voice")
1) Is the tone of the novel humorous? Serious? Sarcastic? Grim? Lofty? Conversational? How can you tell?
2) What does the tone of the novel contribute to its total meaning?
g) Title
1) How does the title relate to, or clarify, the total meaning of the novel?

6. Which of these eight elements of the novel seems to be the most important?
7. Now return to items 1 and 2 and add to your original responses to the novel.

■ Comments on speed reading

Reading rate is an attitude, and such an attitude is seldom improved permanently by external pressure of any kind. Machines and other external devices (for example, a moving hand) designed to increase reading speed are not clearly better than other methods, and they have the major disadvantage that when readers who use external devices read without them, they soon tend to return to their former rate of reading.

The disadvantages of "speed reading" include the following:

1. The pressure to read faster tends to increase the anxiety of students who are already anxious about their reading assignments. As anxiety increases, comprehension usually decreases.
2. Most readers cannot concentrate on their eye movements and on the content of what they are reading at the same time. Therefore, concentration on faster, smoother eye movements usually results in reduced concentration on the content of the reading material.
3. "Speed reading" does not insure clear and accurate initial learning; therefore, it often creates the time-consuming problem of unlearning and relearning.

Improvement in reading speed as well as comprehension is likely to be greater and more lasting if readers try to improve their central processes (perception, comprehension, assimilation) rather than their peripheral processes (eye movements—see Tinker below).

Reading versatility is far more desirable than reading speed. Reading versatility means the ability to adapt reading approach (including rate) to the nature of the reading material and the purpose for which one is reading it. Improvement in reading versatility usually comes with increased background in the subjects about which one usually reads, and with increased attention to setting purposes before beginning to read any material.

> Reading versatility is far
> more desirable than
> reading speed.

For further information on speed reading, consult the following:

Tinker, Miles A. "Role of Eye Movements in Improving Reading," *Bases for Effective Reading*. Minneapolis: University of Minnesota Press, 1965, pp. 105–112.

Whimbey, Arthur and Jack Lochhead. "Six Myths about Reading." *Problem Solving and Comprehension*. 4th rev. ed. Hillsdale, N.J.: L. Erlbaum Assocs., 1986.

C lear and distinct apprehension of the things which we commit to memory," is necessary in order to make them stick and dwell there. . . . If we would treasure up the ideas of things, notions, propositions, arguments and sciences, these should be recommended also to our memory by clear and distinct perception of them. Faint glimmering and confused ideas will vanish like images in twilight.

ISAAC WATTS (1741)

■ Improving Thinking– and Notetaking from Thinking–about the Material You Read

■ Adapting to reading and notetaking in an unfamiliar genre or discipline

A major problem when reading and notetaking in a relatively unfamiliar genre or discipline is deciding what to look for and note as significant. How should you read and take notes from poetry assigned in one of your first literature courses? From legal cases in one of your first law courses? From material assigned in a higher level history or physiology course when you have not had an introductory course in these disciplines? Before considering some specific answers to these questions, consider the following general points:

1. Mere reading or reading and making marks on the page is not an appropriate way to read to learn. To follow many of the "principles of remembering" (listed on pp. 8–9), reading to learn should include making notes of your critical and creative thoughts as they occur to you, and taking notes from the content of the material only when you are fairly sure of what is most significant. (Such "delayed notetaking" is described on pp. 14–15.)

2. If you encounter a word, phrase, sentence, or paragraph you don't understand, pencil a question mark in the margin of the book and keep reading. When you've

come to the end of the material and you return to the question marks, you're likely to have enough perspective and information to comprehend the questioned material more quickly than if you had puzzled over it on the first encounter.

3. Don't be surprised or concerned if your reading in the new genre or discipline is much slower and more laborious than in reading more familiar material. As your familiarity with the new field increases, your comprehension is likely to be quicker and greater. Moreover, freeing yourself of anxiety about being a "slow reader" or "poor reader" will help raise your comprehension; usually, the higher one's anxiety, the lower one's comprehension.

> Mere reading or reading and making marks on the page is not an appropriate way to read to learn.

4. Most important, find out from authorities in the genre or discipline unfamiliar to you what basic questions or structure might guide your initial reading and notetaking. One authority could be a professor in the discipline, who might offer guidance in class or conference, or you might analyze his or her lectures to perceive questions that can guide your reading. Another authority could be a basic current text in the field, or a practitioner or expert beyond the classroom.

5. By starting with a basic current text, you are likely to increase your background in the subject enough that you can read more advanced materials with greater ease. You can read the basic texts selectively; the methodology section and the summary chapter or individual chapter summaries may be sufficient for the purpose of guiding further reading.

For comprehensive recommendations about reading and writing in an unfamiliar discipline or genre, consult a handbook written by an authority in the discipline or genre; for example, *Handbook for Research in American History*, by Francis Paul Purcha (Lincoln: University of Nebraska Press, 1987).

As in all reading and listening, maintain a critical attitude in finding and following a basic structure or questions to guide your reading; that is, be aware that another authority may disagree with the one you've consulted and that you can bring from your own knowledge and experience ideas for expanding or modifying the structure or questions you find.

*I*n the beginning of your application to any new subject, "be not too uneasy under present difficulties that occur, nor too importunate and impatient for answers and solutions to any questions that arise." Perhaps a little more study, a little further acquaintance with the subject, a little time and experience will solve those difficulties, untie the knot, and make your doubts vanish . . .

ISAAC WATTS (1741)

■ Taking notes from textbooks or articles in the biological or physical sciences

In the biological and physical sciences, authorities generally agree about methodology; therefore, almost any authoritative text designed to be an introduction to the science would be appropriate as a source of a structure or questions to guide initial reading. However, before taking an advanced course in the science, a student new to the field will be able to learn more in less time if he reads selectively not only an introductory text to the science but also introductory material regarding the specific area that is the subject of the course.

To study scientific material, follow the suggestions recommended on pages 20–23 for mastering textbook material; in the "reflecting" step, answer the "critical and creative questions" on page 52 which seem most appropriate for your purposes and for the material. For recommendations about studying physics, see "Studying Math and Technical Subjects."

■ Taking notes from history books or articles

History is a field in which there is currently great controversy about methodology. The controversy centers on a difference of opinion among historians about whether history should be classified as one of the humanities or as one of the social sciences. Historians who classify history as one of the humanities tend to regard narrative as the primary method of writing history; those who classify history as a social science tend to regard analysis as the primary method. A student for whom history is an unfamiliar discipline should keep this major difference of opinion in mind as he reads history and perhaps modify the structure or questions that he gains from any one authority to guide his initial reading.

To illustrate, when I asked a history professor to recommend an authoritative book that might guide initial reading of history, I was directed to *Doing History* by J. H. Hexter (Indiana University Press, 1971). When I consulted two more historians for additional ideas to include in this section, I learned that Dr. Hexter's view represents one side of a controversy among historians regarding the relative value of analysis, statistical evidence, and the social sciences in "doing history." Therefore, in using my notes from *Doing History* as a guide in reading history (in this case, *The Emergence of the American University*), I gave more weight to analysis, statistical evidence, and the social sciences than Hexter implies is necessary.

Following are my notes from *Doing History*, a description of the process by which I took notes from one section of *The Emergence of the American University*, and the notes themselves.

Notes from *Doing History* by J. H. Hexter
(Indiana University Press, 1971)

Page
ref.

	Definition of "historiography" ("doing history"):
15	"the craft of writing history and/or the yield of such writing considered in its rhetorical aspect" (Hexter)
154	— as a branch of intellectual history. "the history of the ideas of historians about the past"
15	— as a subbranch of the sociology of knowledge: "the history of history writing."

44	*Thesis:* "The communication and therefore the advancement of historical knowledge is inseparable from the rhetoric of history"; in other words, the historian conveys his knowledge of the past at once by what he writes and by the way he writes.

Basic questions and subquestions that can be derived from *Doing History* to guide initial reading of history:

51	A. How (and how well) has this historian "done" history? (Only "provisional judgments" are possible, even with knowledge of the historical record.)

1. Does the historian communicate what-happened-and-how by historical narrative, historical analysis, or both, organically integrated?

   a) Narrative (telling a story or stories) is "the 27 principle of coherence traditionally and still most generally employed" by historians.

   b) Analysis requires formulation of a rough hypothesis "for which the surviving records hold forth some hope of verification."

2. How "slight or abundant" is the historical evidence, how "adequate or inadequate" the historical proof?

   a) Does the evidence include quantification, 142 statistical foundations? (e.g., "one-fortieth of the population" instead of "a tiny fraction"?)

3. To what extent does the historian use material from the social sciences?

4. To what extent is this history comparative, as opposed to nationalistic or ethnocentric?

5. To what extent is the language denotative, to what extent connotative?

   a) Denotative language of historiography is like that of the natural sciences; it may be desirable and necessary to make accounts more complete, exact.

   Major difference between use of denotative language in history and in natural sciences: "to convey historical reality 57 . with maximum impact may require a historian to subordinate completeness, explicitness, and exactness to other considerations."

   b) Connotative ("evocative and even metaphorical") language of historiography is "nearer to the language of the fictive arts"; it "may be desirable and even necessary," in order to bring the reader "into confron-

43   tation with events long past and men long
            dead," to make accounts "forceful, vivid,
            lively."
                 Major difference between use of con-
            notative language in history and in fic-
            tive arts: the "overriding commitment
47   of historians to fidelity to the surviving
            records of the past."

25   B. What understanding of the past ("historical real-
          ity") does the historian communicate to me
          through his writing?
          — what "movement and tempo of events"
          — what "motives and actions of men"
          — what "impact on the course of events of an ac-
            cident, a catastrophe, or a bit of luck. . . ."?

Description of a Process of Taking Notes from History

Book of history chosen for this description: Lawrence R.
Veysey. *The Emergence of the American University*. Chicago: University of Chicago Press, 1965.

1. I conjectured that the typical assignment in an advanced history course would involve reading from an
   extensive bibliography (rather than mastering one or
   two textbooks), that most of the books in the bibliography would be on reserve in the library, and therefore that the books could not be marked and notes
   would have to be more detailed in order to have sufficient material for review.
2. I read the table of contents to discover the scope of the
   book and to locate the pages where the thesis of the
   book would probably be stated.
3. I looked for a statement of the thesis and elaboration
   of it in the first and last paragraphs of the preface and
   the conclusion; when I found what I was looking for
   (in the first sentence of the opening paragraphs of
   these sections), I noted the pages and parts-of-pages
   from which I would probably want to take notes.

4. Returning to the pages and parts-of-pages I had noted, I took notes on the thesis, quoting directly for the most part (using quotation marks), because the field is relatively new to me and I did not feel certain yet of paraphrasing accurately and quickly.

5. Looking up from my notes, I told myself the thesis from memory in order to impress it more deeply upon my memory and so help me comprehend more quickly as I read on.

6. I returned to the Table of Contents to note the main headings that indicate the scope of the book in relation to the thesis.

7. I decided which section of the book interested me most and was therefore the best place to start reading, because it would help me "get into" the book—connect the material directly with my previous knowledge and interests and so increase my attention and comprehension as I read on.

8. I previewed and then read the section of particular interest to me, "The Academic Standards of the New Age," in the chapter entitled "The Tendency to Blend and Reconcile," noting pages and parts-of-pages from which I might want to take notes.

9. Following the questions suggested to me by Hexter's *Doing History*, modified by what I had learned from other historians, I made notes of my critical response to the section.

10. I took notes on the content of the section. If I were to read the whole book, I would follow steps 8 and 9, then check out the book from the reserve room (overnight or three-day checkout is all that is permitted, usually) and type notes from the content, following my notations of pages and parts of pages.

Note: If I were responsible for mastering the material, I would follow the steps suggested for mastering textbook material (pp. 20–23) to the extent that they seemed necessary.

Notes on the Thesis and Scope of
The Emergence of the American University

Page
ref.

Thesis

439
In America, "the idea of the university . . .
underwent a process . . . of assimilation to the New
World environment, accompanied by profound internal tension and a mingled sense of gain and
loss."

vii
"The most striking thing about the American
university in its formative period is the diversity of
mind shown by the men who spurred its develop-
ment."

viii
"The two most important types of academic
conflict in the late nineteenth century were over the
basic purpose of the new university and over the
kind and degree of control to be exerted by the institution's leadership."

Scope
Part 1:
Rival Conceptions of the Higher Learning,
1865–1910
1. Discipline and Piety
2. Utility
3. Research
4. Liberal Culture
A Season of Reassessment, 1908–1910
Part 2:
The Price of Structure, 1890–1910
5. The Pattern of the New University
(including)
a. The Gulf between Students and
Faculty
b. The Rise of Administration
6. The Tendency to Blend and Reconcile
a. The Growing Merger of Ideals
b. Business Models for Educational
Enterprise

c. The Academic Standards of the
New Age
d. Varieties of the "New"
Administrator
7. The Problem of the Unreconciled
Conclusion:
The University as an American Institution

Notes from One Section*

A. The Academic Standards of the New Age

1. Increasing emphasis on quantification (objected to by some), e.g., Eliot (Harvard): "Quality being secured, the larger the better."
2. "Concern for quantitative success tended to inhibit quality"
   a) Admission standards low in new universities (Cornell, Stanford) to insure numbers
   b) Larger faculty-student ratio made control of academic standards difficult
3. Conflicting evidence re expectations of academic performance
   a) Requirements grew somewhat harder, 1865–1910
      1) More students required to repeat courses
      2) Honors programs instituted
   b) But standards of work very low compared to mid-20th century; e.g., some Harvard students received A's for courses never attended, and only 3 hours of tutoring
4. Improvement of quality difficult because educators disagreed about:
   a) How "serious" undergraduate work should be
   b) "Substantive meaning of seriousness," e.g., scientific vs. humanistic professors; accuracy of footnotes vs. "verbal flair and moral dedication"

---

*Abbreviations are not included here, in order to make the notes more readable; had I abbreviated, I would have used a code like this:

acad. stds. = academic standards	fac. = faculty	st. = students
tchg. = teaching	u. = undergraduates	

Comments on "The Academic Standards of the New Age"

A. Of particular interest and value to me:
  1. The perspective this section gives me on
     a) college admissions problems, past and present (#1 and #2)
     b) past and present need for student services (e.g., learning centers) to help students study more effectively (#3)
     c) current controversy among historians (#4)

B. How Veysey has "done history" here:
  1. Historical analysis; no narrative in this section
     a) Sub-thesis statements supported by extensive evidence (nonstatistical) with many footnotes to indicate direct sources, additional sources, or additional details.
     b) Example: "The standard of work at leading institutions, despite the upturn of the years after 1905, remained extraordinarily low by the canons of the mid-twentieth century. . . . At Yale in 1903 seniors required only an hour or less per day to prepare for all their classes." (Footnote cites three sources of this and of similar information) p. 357
  2. Language almost entirely denotative (as illustrated in quotation above)

C Sense of the past conveyed:
  1. From this section, a sense of the past is largely the result of:
     a) cumulative effect of abundant evidence solidly organized in support of points made
     b) naming rather than narrating of "movement of events," "motives and actions of men"
     c) background that most readers are likely to bring to the book (familiarity with at least one American university)

■ Taking notes from poetry in a first course in literature

To improve your reading and notetaking from poetry, find a basic text on literature in general or on poetry in particular by looking through the books required for introductory courses in literature or poetry. You're likely to learn most readily from introductory books that are clearly organized and relatively free of jargon. On the subject of literature in general, such a book is *A Short Guide to Writing about Literature*, by Sylvan Barnet (5th ed., Glenview, Ill.: Scott Foresman, 1985). On the subject of poetry, such a book is *Introduction to the Poem*, by Robert W. Boynton and Maynard Mack (3rd ed., Portsmouth, N.H.: Boynton/ Cook, 1985).

If you were to take notes from *Introduction to the Poem* to guide your reading of poems, your notes would probably look something like this:

1. Who is the speaker?
2. Who is the audience?
3. What is the tone (of voice) in which the speaker addresses the audience?
4. What is the subject? The theme? The meaning?
5. What does the pattern of rhythm and sound contribute to the effect and meaning of the poem?
6. What "devices of compression" are apparent?
   a) Understatement
   b) Irony
   c) Paradox
   d) Comparison by means of simile, metaphor, juxtaposition
7. How do these devices contribute to the effect and meaning of the poem?

Your notes on your analysis of a specific poem could follow the structure of the questions above. Consider your notes tentative until after you have reread the poem many times to find evidence to support each of your statements, especially those about theme and meaning.

The authors of *Introduction to the Poem* and authors of other introductory texts on literature probably would agree that *before* analyzing a poem in detail you should consider and note the impact of the total poem upon you, and that *after* analyzing a poem you should consider and note the value of the poem for you personally. Questions to guide these initial and final responses might be these:

1. What is the total effect of the poem upon you—emotionally, imaginatively, intuitively, sensually, intellectually?

2. What is the value of the poem for you personally? How has the experience of reading the poem changed you—your attitudes, your feelings, your thinking?

Once you have developed a clear understanding of some of the ways that poems can convey effect and meaning, you will be able to read and take notes from poems more spontaneously, without direct reference to a structure such as the one derived from *Introduction to the Poem*.

Here is an example of notes taken on a poem which follow the structure provided by *Introduction to the Poem*:

Art

Herman Melville

In placid hours well-pleased we dream
Of many a brave unbodied scheme.
But form to lend, pulsed life create,
What unlike things must meet and mate:
A flame to melt—a wind to freeze;
Sad patience—joyous energies;
Humility—yet pride and scorn;
Instinct and study; love and hate;
Audacity—reverence. These must mate,
And fuse with Jacob's mystic heart,
To wrestle with the angel—Art.

1. Immediate total effect: Sense of complexity of art (poetry) and all that contributes to its creation—forces both within and beyond the artist (poet).
2. Elements (and their evidence in the poem):
   a) Dramatic situation: Artist (poet) at once contemplating the act of creating art and engaging in that act. (Evidence: literal and figurative meaning of the words themselves—and their embodiment in a poem.)
   b) Speaker: A dreamer and artist, by implication the creator of this poem on the subject of creating poetry.
   c) Audience: Other dreamers. (Evidence: the grammatical subject and verb of the first two lines are "we dream.")
   d) Tone: (1) Heightening awe (Evidence: the exclamatory fourth line; quickening alternation of various "unlike things" which must mate, from "a flame to melt—a wind to freeze" to "audacity—reverence"; the culminating reference to a mystical story in the Bible); and (2) "audacious" effort. (Evidence: quickening alternation of "unlike things" that must mate and "fuse with Jacob's mystic heart, / To *wrestle* with the angel—Art.")
   e) Rhythm and meter: First five lines are roughly iam-

bic (weak, strong, weak, strong, etc.); the next four
lines are dominated by speech rhythms; the last two
lines return to the iambic. These contrasts support
the contrasts indicated by the words: mere dream-
ing versus the active meeting and mating of "unlike
things"; then the fusing "with Jacob's mystic heart /
to wrestle with the angel—Art."

f) Other sounds: The balance created by the shifts in
rhythm (noted above) is strengthened by a roughly
similar balance in final rhymes: in the first six lines,
every two adjacent lines rhyme; the seventh line is
unrhymed; in the last four lines every two adjacent
lines again rhyme; and lines 3 and 4, 8 and 9 have
matching rhymes. The "mating" of the rhymes
matches the mating described by the words.

3. Devices of compression
   a) Irony: "What unlike things must meet and mate"
   for the creation of art—and how "brave" and not
   so brave is the "unbodied scheme" we dream "in
   placid hours."

   b) Paradox: The creation of art requires both an act of
   love (meeting and mating of "unlike things" within
   the artist) and an act of conflict (fusing "with Jacob's mystic heart, / To *wrestle* with the angel—
   Art").

   c) Main metaphors: (1) Creation of art :: (is analogous to) the act of love by which a child is created
   (lines 3 and 4); (2) work of art :: child, offspring;
   (3) muse of art :: messenger of God, the angel who
   wrestled with Jacob; (4) the artist (poet) :: Jacob.

   d) Juxtaposition: Juxtaposed pairs of unlike things
   suggest the infinite complexity and balance of opposites within human beings and within their cre-
   ations.

4. Subject: The creation of art (poetry). (Evidence: the
   title and the literal and figurative meaning of the
   words of the poem.)

5. Theme: The complex nature of the creative act, requiring all the human faculties and also involvement
   of and with the divine

6. Meaning: Beyond the theme, the poem suggests that the effect upon the artist of creating art is in part similar to the effect upon Jacob of his wrestling with the angel—transformation into a better person.

7. Value for me personally: Effect of the poem: re-creation of the awe of the poet for the creative act, and—through my effort to wrestle with the poem—the realization that reading a poem, like writing one, can be a creative act and so can transform me into a better person. Proof of the truth of the lines by W. H. Auden:

> A poem—a tall story,
> But every good one
> Makes us want to know.

(Know, for instance, the story of Jacob and the angel in Genesis 27–33.)

■ Taking notes from legal cases in a first course in law

If you are unaccustomed to reading legal cases (judicial opinions), you could talk with a practicing attorney to learn appropriate procedures and questions that can guide your reading and notetaking in this field until you have personal or professional purposes to guide your reading.

A practicing attorney would be likely to recommend procedures and questions similar to those that follow:

1. Examine the preface and table of contents of your casebook to see the context of the case you are assigned.

2. Gain some overall view of the case. In an official report, a headnote is usually provided for overview, with one brief paragraph for each point in the judicial opinion. (Don't depend on headnotes for accuracy, however.) In a law-school casebook, which does not have headnotes, you can usually get an overview by reading the concluding paragraph of the case and then reading, from the beginning, the first sentence of each paragraph (the first and last sentence of every long paragraph).

3. Read the entire case, chunking the material and taking notes after reading each chunk, according to the following structure:

a) Facts

What are the facts of the case? What happened between the parties? Note the facts very briefly.

b) Nature of the action and procedural status

1) What is the nature of the action? How did the case get to court? Three examples of the many possibilities here are "A sued B for damages," "A was prosecuted by the state for the crime of _____," or "A sued B for injunctive relief."

2) What is the procedural status of the case? Two examples of the many possibilities here are "A got a verdict of _____; B appealed the verdict to a higher court on the basis of _____," or "Plaintiff appealed from the granting of a motion to dismiss his action."

c) Issue or question

What is the central issue or question raised in this case? (There may be more than one question or issue.) For example, in People vs. Tomlins, the case briefed on the next pages, the central issue is, "Does a person have the right to kill in self-defense when attacked in his own home and when safe retreat is available?"

d) Decision of the court

1) What is the conclusion or holding of the court? (The "court" in some cases will be one judge; in other cases, as many as nine judges.)

2) By what reasoning did the court arrive at its conclusion?

3) What is the rule of law on which the conclusion is based? (The rule of law usually will be the answer to the central issue or question; it is the legal principle for which the case stands.)

e) Your critical questions or comments

What do you think about the case?

4 Your notes for each case should be limited to one side of one page or card, and they should have the same structure (roughly, (a) facts, (b) nature of the action

and procedural status, (c) issue or question, (d) decision of the court, (e) your critical questions or comments) so that you can compare quickly and directly your notes from many similar cases to draw conclusions about a particular body of law.

5. Buy a legal dictionary to consult for precise definitions of terms that you encounter in your reading.

Once you have developed familiarity with court opinions, you should be able to read and take notes according to an order or system related to your specific purpose for reading a case.

Some law schools may have orientation days that include presentations or materials regarding effective ways to read legal cases. Such materials have been developed at the University of Pennsylvania by Professor Louis B. Schwartz. In his mimeographed booklet, "Studying Law for Fun and Profit" (1978), Professor Schwartz describes first the goals of legal education:

Legal education aims to develop critical judgment and a particular set of professional skills. Among these skills are careful reading and precise writing, the power to analyze an argument, differentiating facts from opinion, and recognizing the basic premise or assumption from which the argument proceeds.

In the extract below, Professor Schwartz provides a sample of appropriate notetaking from a legal case, which in part illustrates the above recommendations and in part illustrates that good notetaking by law students can vary slightly so long as the focus is on the *legal issues* involved in the case.

People vs. Tomlins (N.Y. 1914)

Facts: T shot his son in their home. Testified he acted in s.d. and provoked by blows. Judge charged df. had a duty to retreat if possible where there was a reasonably safe means of escape, rather than kill. Jury conv. T of 1st deg. murder.

Question on Appeal: Did the court commit reversible error in so instructing?

Decision and Reasons: Rev'd. because of erroneous instr. No duty to retreat when attacked in one's home. "Flight is for sanctuary and shelter, and shelter, if not sanctuary, is in the home." Ct. follows Ala. decision in holding that it makes no difference whether attacker was another occupant rather than intruder. Dictum that duty to retreat exists only in "sudden affrays."
Error held rev'bl. even tho def. atty. did not object, since charge in effect deprived T of jury trial. Statute allows reversal in capital case where "justice requires."

Rule: Not criminal to kill in s.d. when attacked in one's own home even if safe retreat available and even if attacker also lives in same home.

Comment: Wouldn't more lives be saved if retreat were required in such situations? Query as to duty to retreat *only* in "sudden affrays." Maybe ruling requiring retreat from murderous attack when man has means of defense is inconsistent with human nature.

Professor Schwartz then comments on these notes as follows:

Note use of abbreviations to save time. The "Question on Appeal" and "Rule" are not absolutely essential since it is fairly obvious from the facts and the decision what the questions are and what rule the case could be cited for. Note the quoted words from Cardozo's opinion. This was not essential either, but occasionally it is worth taking note of a striking statement which embodies the rule or policy that seems to influence the court. The "Comment" heading is where you put your own original reaction to the decision. *Always carry your thinking about a case far enough to have a definite sense of agreement or disagreement with the court's judgment.* Test the court's "rule" by thinking of cases where literal application would make it absurd. Formulate an alternative rule which might be enacted by statute. Test its possibilities for absurd application.

Be sure to note reference to statutes in an opinion. Did the language of the statute compel the judge to decide as he did? Was the statute intended to codify the common law or to change it? Which were the crucial words that the Court had to interpret?

The foregoing recommendations for reading and notetaking in studying poetry or the law are examples of the recommendations you can find for any genre or discipline if you consult an expert or an introductory text by an expert in the field. Keep in mind that notes from the same material could be taken according to a different organization or system, depending upon your academic or personal purposes beyond basic comprehension. In fact, changing the organization or system can be valuable in itself, because it can result in your having a new understanding of, or realization about, the subject.

Remember that your business in reading or in conversation, especially on the subject of natural, moral, or divine science, is not merely to know the opinion of the author or speaker, for this is but the mere knowledge of history; but your chief business is to consider whether their opinions are right or no, and to improve your own solid knowledge of that subject by meditation on the themes of their writing or discourse. Deal freely with every author you read, and yield up your assent only to evidence and just reasoning on the subject.

ISAAC WATTS (1741)

■ Questioning to encourage critical and creative reading of any expository (factual or theoretical) material

The following questions can serve as a useful stock from which to draw in thinking about and taking notes on expository material. To increase your interest, attention, and memory, your initial question should be, "What in this material is of particular interest to me?"

1. Critical questions: analysis
   a) What authority or credentials does the author bring to the subject?
   b) What does the author state?
   c) What does the author imply? Assume?
   d) Is the argument valid (internally consistent, logical; do the conclusions follow from the premises)?
   e) Is the argument reliable (supported by evidence, authentic)?
   f) Does the form strengthen or support the content (by being clear, concise, coherent)?
2. Creative questions: synthesis and elaboration
   a) How does the material relate to:
      1) my own experience, opinion, knowledge?
      2) other sources, oral or written, on a similar subject
         i) from other schools or other fields?
         ii) based on other paradigms or other theories?

iii) by other authors in the same school or field?
   b) What additions can I think of (improvements, more
      evidence, additional arguments, new questions)?
3. Creative questions: applications
   a) What applications can I think of?
   b) For whom might this have value?
   c) How can this change *me*?

To increase your interest, attention, and memory, your initial question should be, "What in this material is of particular interest to me?"

■ Minding metaphors

Metaphors, one of the "devices of compression" characteristic of poetry, may be found in any writing except purely scientific or mathematical material. Metaphor may cause comprehension problems for readers who are not alert to this way of conveying meaning.

A metaphor (derived from the Greek words for "beyond"—*meta*— and "bear" or "carry"—*phor*) bears meaning beyond the literal level. If you think of the same word as it might be found in purely scientific and in purely poetic material, you are likely to appreciate more fully the way that metaphor bears meaning.

Consider the differences between the meaning of words like "light" and "fire" in scientific material and the meaning of the same words in poetry.

In scientific material:

> The sun is our most important source of light.
> Fire is the heat and light that come from burning substances.

In a poem by Dylan Thomas:

> Do not go gentle into that good night,
> Rage, rage against the dying of the light.

In a poem by John Masefield:

> Be with me, Beauty, for the fire is dying;
> My dog and I are old, too old for roving. . . .
> Only stay with me while the mind remembers
> The beauty of fire from the beauty of embers.

With these quotations in view, consider language as a continuum from the purely scientific to the purely poetic, as shown in the following figure.

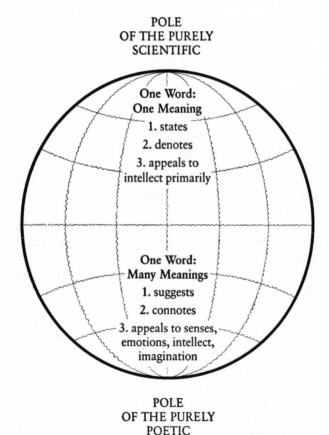

POLE
OF THE PURELY
SCIENTIFIC

One Word:
One Meaning

1. states

2. denotes

3. appeals to
intellect primarily

One Word:
Many Meanings

1. suggests

2. connotes

3. appeals to senses,
emotions, intellect,
imagination

POLE
OF THE PURELY
POETIC

The continuum of language shown suggests that written material may be located at any point from the purely scientific to the purely poetic; that is, that it may be more or less scientific or poetic. In reading any material, especially material in a genre or discipline new to you, be alert to metaphors and the meanings they convey. Also notice similes, "figures of comparison" like metaphors, but ones that are pointed out directly by the author.

> Be alert to metaphors and the meanings they convey.

Here are examples of metaphors and similes found in material representative of several different disciplines:

History
A historian should yield himself to his subject, become immersed in the place and period of his choice, standing apart from it now and then for a fresh view; as a navigator, after taking soundings off a strange coast, retires to peruse his charts and then emerges to give the necessary orders to continue the voyage safely.

Samuel E. Morison
in *Vistas of History*

Psychiatry
The problem of anxiety neurosis may be epitomized metaphorically as an overactive "alarm system." The anxious patient is so keyed to the possibility of harm that he is constantly warning himself about potential dangers. . . . Almost any stimulus may be sufficient to trip off the warning system and create a "false alarm." The consequence . . . is that the patient does experience harm—he is in a constant state of anxiety.

Aaron T. Beck
in *Cognitive Therapy and the Emotional Disorders*

Linguistics
A game of chess is like an artificial realization of what language offers in a natural form . . . a state of the set of

chessmen corresponds closely to a state of language. The respective value of the pieces depends on their position on the chessboard just as each linguistic term derives its value from its opposition to all other terms.

Ferdinand de Saussure
in *Course in General Linguistics*

In addition to such incidental metaphors and similes, basic and pervasive metaphors can be found in almost every field. For example, in the field of English literature, the metaphor of a plant (usually a tree) has been used to convey the concept of "organic form." According to the theory of organic form, a work of art "grows like a living organism, its parts inseparable and indivisible, and the whole being greater than the sum of its parts. . . ." (C. Hugh Holman, in *A Handbook to Literature*.)

Minding the metaphor of a tree can be helpful in trying to analyze a literary work. In the field of psychology, perhaps the most well-known metaphor is that of the computer as an information processing mechanism comparable to the human mind. In education, the process of education in general (and reading in particular) has for centuries been compared to nourishment, as it is in this quotation from Alfred North Whitehead (*The Aims of Education and Other Essays*):

> It must never be forgotten that education is not a process of packing articles in a trunk. . . . Its nearest analogue is the assimilation of food by a living organism: and we all know how necessary to health is palatable food under suitable conditions. When you have put your boots in a trunk, they will stay there till you take them out again; but this is not at all the case if you feed a child with the wrong food.

■ Preparing a Research Paper

To meet the due date, schedule on your calendar when you will *start* each of the following major steps by counting back from the date your paper is due and estimating approximately how many days you should allow for each step. Until you are experienced in preparing research papers, shorten the time for each major step by seeking help from a university writing center or a professional writing consultant.

■ Research

1. Choose your topic carefully.
   a) Jot down as many topics as you can think of related to a subject that is appropriate or actually assigned for your paper.
   b) Evaluate the topics you've listed, considering especially your genuine personal interest in the topic and its likely value for you.
   c) Limit and organize your topic both before and during your research on it. To decide what to include, consider what you know and want to know about the topic, what the instructor has assigned, and how much time you have to complete the paper.
      1) Build your paper around a question, for which the paper serves as a well-balanced and well-organized answer, with all the necessary evidence to support your points.
      2) Or, develop and defend a potent idea or thesis about the subject with explicit reference to alter-

native views and possibilities, which you should research carefully and fairly.

2. Write a list of as many questions as you can think of about your topic. Study the questions to:
   a) find possible categories that might be included in your paper;
   b) eliminate questions that are likely to take you too far from your central topic.

> Build your paper around a question . . . or develop and defend a potent idea or thesis about the subject.

3. Get an overview of your topic by reading a general source, such as an encyclopedia article, and note names, events, terms, or ideas that you might use in your library search for specific sources.

4. Locate and note information sources efficiently.
   a) Take advantage of the information sheets on library use and services that are available in your library. Use the library's printed guides and take a tour to learn how the library is organized and whether there are any special collections or departmental libraries in your subject area.
   b) Revise your list of subject headings or key words to use in researching your topic. Ask the reference librarians for advice at this stage; they can suggest headings to use as well as sources to consult.
   c) Locate appropriate books through the library's catalog. This may be a card catalog, an on-line (computerized) catalog, or a combination of both.
      1) From the catalog, note on separate notepad pages the author, title, location, and call number of all books that seem likely to contain useful information. In making your choices, notice the

date of publication and the scope and tone indicated by the title.

2) Find and look over each promising book to determine further its possible usefulness. Check the table of contents and the index, the qualifications of the author, and the degree of scholarship indicated on an aspect of the subject you are relatively familiar with.

3) Indicate in an upper corner of the bibliographical slip the status of the book, e.g., "not in the library," "not useful," "being called in," or other information, and group the slips accordingly.

d) Check the periodical indexes in the reference room for current journal, magazine, and newspaper articles on your subject. This is another point at which a reference librarian can help you plan your work. Some libraries offer computerized literature searching. There may be a fee for this service, but it can often provide an extensive list of references on your subject and save you a great amount of time.

e) Write a full bibliographical card* only for those

---

* *Books*: Author, title, edition, place of publication, publisher, date of publication. *Articles*: Author, article title, periodical title, volume, date, pages.

books and periodicals from or about which you expect to take notes. Use standard bibliographical form, as discussed below.

    f) If important materials on your topic are not accessible, *consider changing your topic.*

5. Read portions of the books appropriate to the subject and make page notations and notes of your ideas about the material.

    a) As you read, note the pages and parts-of-pages (A, B, C, D, E) from which you think you'll want to take notes when you complete most of your reading; make these notations on the bibliographical card for the book (see page 14).

    b) Note on separate cards each of your own original ideas regarding the subject, indicating the author and page number of the material about which you are commenting.

6. Ordinarily, do *not* take notes *yet* from the content itself. *Arrange for a conference with your professor* when you have read enough to know one or two theses or questions that seem promising bases for your paper. You can save immeasurable time and effort and insure the success of your paper if you discuss your plans at this point, with your professor or supervisor.

7. Write a tentative and very brief outline that you can draw from for the headings on each note card.

8. Take notes from your reading.

    a) Return to the pages you've noted and, if the material still seems valuable in view of the thesis you have decided upon, take notes of some kind: summary, quotations, paraphrase.

    b) Use a separate card for each new idea. Include a note of the subject in the upper right-hand corner and the author and the exact page reference in the upper left-hand corner.

    c) Take great care to avoid plagiarism and infringement of copyright. For well-illustrated guidance in avoiding plagiarism, see *A Handbook for Writers*, 4th ed., by Wilfred Stone and J. G. Bell (New York: McGraw-Hill, 1983). For detailed guidance in avoiding copyright infringement, see a library or legal reference book, such as *Copyright Law: A Practitioner's Guide*, 2nd ed., by Harry G. Henn (New York: Practising Law Institute, 1988, supp. 1989), brief excerpts of which are provided in the appendix of this book.

9. It is very important that you add to your notes your critical appraisal and original ideas about the material, noting the author and the page number of the material you are commenting about.

10. Use your ingenuity to discover other possible sources of information in addition to books and periodicals: for example, individuals informed on the subject, and your personal experience.

11. Compile clear definitions of all important terms.

12. Keep notepad pages or index cards handy for noting ideas that may come to you in odd moments, and add these to your collection of notes.

■ Write

1. First of all, use a word processor if at all possible. This miracle machine of the 1980s is an invaluable aid to efficient and effective thinking and writing.

2. Prepare a brief statement of the thesis, purpose, and/or scope of your paper to serve as a point of reference to keep you close to your subject as you write.

3. Write a full outline, following the steps below:
   a) Arrange your notes carefully in what seems to be an appropriate sequence.
   b) Include definitions of key terms.
   c) Add cards with notes of any new ideas, insights, and conclusions that come to you as you review all the notes that you have taken from your readings.
   d) From your note cards, write your outline in sentence form, to insure clarity and continuity as you write your paper from it.

4. Write a first draft of your paper.
   a) Review comments by professors or supervisors on your previous papers for ideas that can improve your current paper.
   b) Write point by point from your outline, reorganiz-

ing when it seems desirable; write the introduction later if it seems difficult to express at first.

c) In footnotes or endnotes, give credit to (cite) all sources of ideas and quotations not your own. (See 8(c) under "Research," above.)

d) Consult current standard style manuals for an appropriate and consistent form for footnotes and bibliography. (Use the *MLA Handbook*, *Manual for Biological Journals*, *American Psychological Association Publications Manual*, or other appropriate style manuals.) (See Bibliography.)

e) Strive for fluent expression, not precise diction, in this draft; bracket words that you think should be replaced in later drafts.

f) Concentrate on writing a strong introduction and conclusion. The introduction should state your thesis or question clearly; the conclusion should include a brief summary and restatement of the thesis or question.

■ Revise

1. After completing your first draft, and making a printout if you are using a word processor, wait at least a day to allow time for mental refreshment. Then reread and polish the draft.

a) Check: Are your points clear? Does every paragraph develop the thesis? Is the progression logical and coherent?

b) Find the precise words that express your points.

    c) Reread parts of the paper aloud to reveal possible rough spots in the form.

    d) In a long paper, provide additional organizational aids for the reader (for example, a table of contents and headings).

2. Write a second draft of the pages that need major revision, or make another printout, and allow time for mental refreshment again. (Several revisions may be desirable, if time is available.)

3. Type or print out a final draft. Proofread and correct the final draft; run a final copy if you are using a word processor.

4. Be sure to print a spare, or make a copy by carbon or photocopy, for your own safekeeping.

■ Submit

Turn the paper in on time (or, if absolutely necessary, arrange for a new deadline that is possible for you to meet and acceptable to your professor or supervisor)

■ Using Four Methods for Effective Study and for Analogous Activities

Many of the preceding sections of this book referred to four basic and interdependent methods of improving reading, writing, and study: previewing, selecting, chunking, and deep processing.

The four methods can be applied to lengthy as well as brief activities, to taking round-the-world trips and writing dissertations or preparing for comprehensive examinations as well as to taking short trips and studying single chapters. For an extended study task, previewing involves determining carefully the scope of the task. Selecting and chunking involve dividing the whole into parts and deciding which tasks to work on first and which to work on most thoroughly, and grouping the tasks that can be done best in close relationship. Deep processing involves studying one chunk after another, using the ways of thinking about the material that are most appropriate for each chunk and for your purposes.

Naturally, previewing, selecting, chunking, and deep processing are not always necessary or desirable. They *are* necessary and desirable when efficiency is important, and when the major purpose is accomplishment of some kind within limited time and in a competitive situation—the conditions of most academic work. For other activities, one or two of the methods might be desirable or useful but not all four. For instance, when you're on vacation you may enjoy simply wandering, without studying a map of the area, and when you come upon a shelf of books you may enjoy simply choosing a book on whim and wandering through it.

Here is a graphic summary of the *Four Methods Basic to Effective Study*:

Four Methods Basic to Effective Study

Preview
Preview books that you need to study for an exam or to write a research paper.

Preview
Preview the chapter most interesting to you or most appropriate for your purposes.

Select
Select the book most interesting or appropriate to start with, preferably one providing an overview of the subject.

Select
Select the part of the chapter most interesting or appropriate to read first.

Chunk
Chunk by grouping the books according to subject, author, or other aspect related to your purposes.

Chunk
Chunk by grouping parts of the chapter according to problems to be solved or questions to be answered or according to sections appropriate for notetaking. Read one chunk at a time.

Process
Process the book in ways most appropriate for your purposes, such as outlining answers to anticipated exam questions or making notes for a research paper.

Process
After reading a chunk, process in ways most appropriate for your purposes: reciting what you have learned or solving a problem or answering a question, or noting ideas about the material and pages and parts-of-pages from which to take notes of the content eventually.

■ Developing a Habit or Hobby of Strengthening Vocabulary

1. When reading or listening, write every unfamiliar word on an index card.
   a) Note the phrase in which you found the word (or the page and part-of-page—indicated by A, B, C, D, E—noting the phrase later).
   b) Guess the meaning from the context of the word and from structural clues, but do not write down your guess. Read on.
2. After collecting a number of words, add to each index card (using a good dictionary)* the following information:
   a) any part of the pronunciation you're not sure about;
   b) phrase in which you found the word (with quotation marks);
   c) derivation, if it will help you remember the meaning;
   d) meaning appropriate for the context quoted;
   e) other useful meanings, synonyms and antonyms;
   f) definitions of unfamiliar synonyms or antonyms (to clarify any subtle differences between these and the key word);

---

* For studying in your major field or at a level above that of an introductory course in a discipline new to you, you should own a current, authoritative dictionary specific to the field; for example, in literature, C. Hugh Holman's *Handbook to Literature* (Odyssey Press).

    g) other forms of the word;

    h) word on the back of the card for drill purposes.

3. Study new words in odd moments, thinking of ways you might use them in actual contexts. For each word:

    a) study the spelling, definition, and any other information you have noted about the word;

> **Study new words in odd moments, thinking of ways you might use them in actual contexts.**

    b) write the word from memory; check immediately for accuracy;

    c) recite the definition and other information from memory; check immediately for accuracy.

Here are two examples of vocabulary cards that I have accumulated since I began the hobby of word collecting years ago. I include them here to illustrate that notetaking about words researched can be very brief, including only information that can help you understand, remember, and want to use the word.

---

euphoric

"The experience [Harvard] tends to be more astringent than *euphoric*"

From Greek "eu" = well
        + "phoric" = to bear

"giving a sense of well being and buoyancy; incapable of depression or readily shaking it."

<u>heuristic</u>
- "start with it as a heuristic principle"
- "the use of the heuristic hunch"
From Greek, "to discover" - EUREKA!
"serving to find out (for oneself),
such as an educational system in
which student is trained to find
out things for self."

■ Learning a Foreign Language

In learning a foreign language, you can apply or adapt many of the ideas in the preceding sections, beginning with "Remembering Effectively," "Mastering Textbook Material" (under "Developing Reading Versatility"), and "Strengthening Vocabulary." Other sections of this book can help you read, write, and study in a foreign language as well as in your native language.

However, learning a foreign language requires additional methods and effort:

1. Use audiotapes regularly; these accompany most textbooks for foreign-language study.
2. Study frequently—six days a week—in short, intensive sessions.
3. In learning new words, cluster or group about five words that are related in some way; then study the words one cluster at a time.
4. Study most intensively the words and phrases that you find most difficult to remember.
   a) Use as many senses, in as many ways as you can, while thinking. For example: write the word or phrase while looking at it and saying it, think about its parts and its meaning, write it again while saying it but not looking at it, check to see if you got it right. Repeat this process several times.
   b) Look for some way to relate the difficult word to something familiar, and think of this relationship as you continue to rehearse the word.
   c) Write the word or phrase on index cards, as de-

scribed in "Strengthening Vocabulary," and review the cards orally several times a day, in odd moments, and before you go to sleep the night before a test.

5. Read passages for their general meaning, without concern for recognizing every word. When you encounter an unfamiliar word, write it on a 3×5 memo page or index card. When you have finished reading the passage, decide which words you need to learn, and proceed to learn them by following the method described above, in #2 and #3.

6. Look for opportunities to use the foreign language in real-life situations or with other students of the language. Use it for greetings and for expressing ideas and thoughts that are important to you. Rehearse for real-life use by imagining situations that involve several speakers and playing all the roles. Read current foreign-language newspapers and magazines and see

foreign-language films. Learn songs in the language and sing them aloud. Try to visit places where the language is spoken widely. Such real-life use can enhance your motivation and increase your learning in ways no other method can.

> Look for opportunities to use the foreign language in real-life situations.

If you have severe problems mastering a foreign language, you might need special help. Usually this involves more repetition and more time to learn the language. Seek help through your instructor, the faculty member responsible for language instruction in your school, a learning center, and/or an office for students who are disabled (including learning disabled).

■ Improving Writing

If you look back in this book, you will see that there is only one section, "Preparing a Research Paper," which is directly about writing. The rest of the sections are more directly about reading. But reading and writing, speaking and listening, are related in many ways, so that some of the ways to improve each can also be applied to improving the others.

The relationships between reading and writing and ways to improve them can be made clearer by using the same terms for their similar aspects. For example, we could say that in reading expository writing we look for a *thesis* and ways by which it is supported, while in writing we develop a *thesis* statement and ways to support it. Similarly, we could use the terms *previewing*, *selecting*, *chunking*, and *deep processing*, which are described on pages 64–65 as ways to improve reading, in describing ways to improve writing.

Here, then, are direct suggestions for ways you can improve your writing, in terms of the ways recommended for improving reading. In writing as in reading, the activities are interrelated or overlap. While reading is like eating a dinner, writing is like creating a dinner. It usually involves some step-by-step activities, but mostly it involves back-and-forth considering and doing, reconsidering and revising, until just before the guests sit down to eat.

■ Prepare to write

1. Collect as much material as you can about your subject before you try to write a first draft. For a research paper, this should involve the kind of reading and notetaking described in "Preparing a Research Paper."

2. Make notes of your ideas and observations. To save time, write each idea or observation on separate small pages or cards, so that you can arrange and rearrange them before you write your first draft.

■ Preview

Previewing is helpful at several times during the writing process but especially after you've collected as much material as you can and before you write your first draft.

1. Preview all the notes that you have accumulated on your subject.
2. If the genre in which you're to write is unfamiliar to you, ask your instructor, a librarian, or another authority to recommend a model of the genre to examine so that you can get a good sense of the structure of it.
3. At some point as you were preparing to write, you may have developed a question or idea about the subject which guided you as you made notes; if not, you should try to think of such a question or idea as you preview. At the same time, look for relationships among the ideas you have accumulated which might contribute to answering your question or supporting your idea or thesis.

■ Select and chunk

Sort and group your notes according to the relationships you see as you preview:

1. *Select* by deciding on a question or thesis and the most promising way to answer the question or support the thesis.
2. Select the audience for which you want to write, and keep that audience in mind as you write and revise, to make what you say and how you say it as appropriate as possible. In an academic situation, the audience is mainly the instructor; keep your particular instructor in mind.
3 Sort out from your notes all those that are appropriate

for the question or thesis and the audience you have selected.

4. *Chunk* by sketching a pattern—a map or an outline—to represent your decisions about how you will group and arrange your ideas.

5. Write your outline in full sentences. These sentences should be the main assertions that you feel ready to make in answer to your question or in support of your thesis. Keep in mind that you may change these assertions as you continue to write.

■ Process deeply

1. Write your paper following your map or outline and your notes. Feel free to reconceive and reorder your ideas as you see new relationships or even discover a better question or a more potent thesis.

2. You will have processed deeply in preparing to write and in previewing, selecting, and chunking. You will be continuing to process deeply as you write, as you revise your paper, and when at last you read your finished product. Because deep processing occurs throughout the writing process, writing is regarded as a way of knowing or getting to know, not just a way of telling.

> Writing is regarded as a way of knowing . . . not just a way of telling.

3. Revise your draft and rewrite until you feel satisfied enough with your product to show it to a friend.

4. Ask your friend to respond to a particular part of your writing which you are concerned about. Revise your writing in the light of any of the friend's suggestions that seem right to you.

5. In some schools or departments or classes, this sort of sharing of papers may not be appropriate or accept-

able. When this is the case, allow several days between each rereading of your drafts and read them as if you were the audience for whom you have written.

6. Examine each draft for ways to make it more easily previewable by your readers and clearer and more readable in style.

7. Edit your final draft; weed out redundancies, imprecisions, and errors in grammar or spelling. Realize that you will find ways to improve your paper whenever you reread it; it will never be perfect—and it need not be. Just do your best in the time you have.

To illustrate the process I have recommended, I will describe how I wrote these pages, imperfect as they must be.

To prepare to write them, I noted on 3 × 5 memo pages all the ideas that came to my mind about ways to write more effectively, particularly for academic purposes. I read or reviewed half a dozen books about writing, noting pages and parts-of-pages from which I might want to take notes eventually. As I read, I noted my own new ideas about my subject immediately, each idea on a separate memo page.

When I felt I had done enough reading or reviewing for my purposes, I returned to my notations of pages and parts-of-pages and made notes from each book on separate 3 × 5 pages, noting the author and page number in the upper left corner.

When I felt I had accumulated enough notes and ideas, I previewed all my notes, looking for relationships among them and ways that they might best be arranged to answer the question, "What suggestions should I give to students for improving the way they go about their writing?" As I previewed, I wrote additional notes when new ideas occurred to me. I also began to sort the note pages into stacks and I jotted down headings for each stack. Here are the headings I jotted down:

Reading related to writing
Previewing
Selecting
Chunking
Deep processing
Books about improving writing

Then I wrote a first draft of the assertions I felt I could make and ways that I might support the assertions. Here is what I wrote:

As reading and writing are related, so are ways to improve them.
Previewing, selecting, chunking, and deep processing can be applied to writing as well as to reading.
Explain application.
Illustrate.
Read books about improving writing.

Following this rough outline and my matching stacks of notes, I wrote a first draft. I set the draft aside for about a week. When I reread the draft I marked revisions directly on it. A week later I copied the revised draft, editing as I typed.

I read the draft aloud to myself and made more changes. I duplicated the revised second draft so that I could show it to one of my colleagues, Susan L. Lytle. Susan suggested that I revise the pages to build up the part about preparing to write, make more statements about improving writing, and weed out some of the details of my explanations. She also suggested that I illustrate the process I was recommending by using some other writing than the pages themselves. I followed the first three suggestions, but I decided not to follow the last one.

In my first draft I realized, to my surprise, that I had forgotten my main audience. I seemed to be writing for teachers, who are the audience for most of my professional writing, rather than students. When I wrote the second draft I kept in mind an audience of students or a particular student and also the structure and metaphors I had used for the first edition of this "ways to" book for students. I typed a third draft of the pages, edited them briefly, and read the draft aloud to myself. I made additional changes indicated by the way my words sounded when I read them aloud.

I duplicated the third draft to show to several more of my colleagues. They pointed out sentences that I could make clearer or more concise.

I typed a fourth draft and sent this to my editor, Bob Boynton. Bob suggested that I be more realistic or frank in making some of my points; for example, I should admit that the only audience for most academic writing "is the teacher, unfortunately."

The result of the process I have just described is the section of *More Learning in Less Time* that you are reading now.

Learning to use a word processor, which I did between the second and third editions of this book, has enhanced my life and writing. Using this magical machine saves immeasurable time and makes the writing process so much more pleasurable and the product so much more readable that it actually helps prevent procrastination and increase concentration.

Buy or rent a word processor if you can, or arrange to use one regularly through the computer resource center at your institution.

For more ideas about ways to improve your writing, look for books on the subject which seem consistent with the way you like to work. To find them, look in college book shops on the shelves labeled for English composition courses, and consult teachers of writing for their recommendations.

Here are some books about improving writing that are recommended highly:

Belanoff, Pat, et al. *The Right Handbook*. Portsmouth, N.H.: Heinemann-Boynton/Cook, 1986.

Berthoff, Ann E., with James Stephens. *Forming/Thinking/Writing*. 2nd ed. Portsmouth, N.H.: Heinemann-Boynton/Cook, 1988.

Brannon, Lil, et al. *Writers Writing*. Portsmouth, N.H.: Heinemann-Boynton/Cook, 1982.

Elbow, Peter. *Writing Without Teachers*. New York: Oxford University Press, 1973.

Flower, Linda. *Problem Solving Strategies For Writing*. 2nd ed. San Diego: Harcourt, 1985

Kaye, Sanford. *Writing Under Pressure: The Quick Writing Process*. New York: Oxford University Press, 1989.

Macrorie, Ken. *The I-Search Paper*. Portsmouth, N.H.: Heinemann-Boynton/Cook, 1988.

Schwartz, Mimi. *Writing for Many Roles*. Portsmouth, N.H.: Heinemann-Boynton/Cook, 1985.

Stone, Wilfred and J. G. Bell. *Prose Style: A Handbook for Writers*. 4th ed. New York: McGraw-Hill, 1983.

Williams, Joseph. *Style: Ten Lessons in Clarity and Grace*. 3rd ed. Glenview, Ill.: Scott Foresman, 1988.

■ Preparing for Examinations

The best preparation for examinations is regular study, including reviewing and learning class notes after every lecture or two, and mastering each textbook assignment on first reading it.

Special review, beginning at least a few days before the exam, is also necessary.

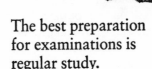

The best preparation for examinations is regular study.

1. Plan a realistic study schedule and stick to it as closely as possible.
   a) Decide how much material you must review and approximately how long one unit of it will take; divide the number of units over the time available, and note this on your calendar.
   b) Distribute study time over at least two sessions for minor tests and at least four for major exams. Review periods should be relatively brief, because recalling and organizing ideas is so fatiguing that ef-

ficiency usually decreases rapidly after about an hour of review.

2. If a problem or plan in another area of your life is distracting, keep paper handy for noting ideas or feelings that occur to you about the problem or plan; wait until a study break to think more about them. (See the section on "Improving Concentration," p. 96.)

3. Study *actively*.

   a) Begin by quickly previewing all your class notes and making a one-page outline (a table of contents) for them.

   b) Study as a unit each subject within the course, for example, all notes from all sources on the same subject.

      1) Treat your class notes as you would treat a textbook chapter. After reviewing your table of contents, review and recite one section (one chunk) at a time.

      2) Review your one-page outline for each textbook chapter and then recite or write briefly from memory; reread portions of the textbook *only* if you can't remember the supporting details well; they should come to your mind as you encounter each cue on your outline.

      3) Prepare and study a master outline of important portions of the subject for which lectures, textbooks, and supplementary reading interrelate

   > Create graphic aids to help you understand and remember the material; for example, a time line, an outline map, a model of a theory.

   c) Create graphic aids to help you understand and remember the material; for example, a time line, an outline map, a model of a theory

d) While reading and reviewing, build a list of page and part-of-page references (A, B, C, D, E) about major terms or concepts. In reviewing for exams, take notes from these page references on separate notepad pages. Arrange the pages for each term or

concept in an appropriate order for a comprehensive definition.

e) Build a list of terms, using indentation to show relationships among them. Fold the list in half lengthwise; think through the definition of each term; for definitions you find hard to remember, write the definitions briefly on the righthand side of the list.

f) Avoid artificial (that is, insignificant) mnemonic (memory) devices because these cannot help you understand the material. Instead, group key terms or ideas in significant ways. See examples of both significant and insignificant mnemonic devices on pages 83–84.

g) Write down any questions or ideas that come to your mind about the material you are reviewing.

1) In particular, use your imagination and your knowledge of controversies in the field you are studying to change the point of view from which you think about the subject.

    2) Make notes of your new insights.

    3) Use all your personal notes in steps 3 and 4.

h) For an essay exam, make up exam questions or ask your professor if old exam questions are available and think through or roughly outline your answers to the questions. (Do this no later than two days before the exam.)

    1) Anticipate one or two very broad questions. As you review your notes, write down points and pages appropriate for an answer to the question(s).

    2) Cooperate with a friend in making up and exchanging more limited (and more likely) exam questions; in a dress-rehearsal situation, outline your answers to the friend's questions; later, discuss your answers with your friend.

    3) Build a structure by which to recall key ideas that you are likely to need quickly—for example, the elements to consider in analyzing a poem or a painting, or the factors to consider in analyzing a problem in economics.

i) Pretend to teach—or actually arrange to tutor— portions of the subject on which you will be examined. Tutoring usually results in the teacher learning more than the student (some of the probable reasons may be found in the section on "Remembering Effectively," page 8).

4. Allow time to pay special attention to the parts of the material that you have found hardest.

   a) Testing yourself will help you find your weak spots; work on these most.

   b) Just before going to sleep on the night before the exam, review the hardest parts, your master outlines, and your outlines of answers to the questions that you or your friend have anticipated.

5. Get adequate sleep two nights before the exam (in case you have any problem sleeping the next night), and the night before the exam (so that you can think as clearly as possible while taking the exam).

*T*alking over the things which you have read with your companions on the first proper opportunity you have for it, is a most useful manner of review or repetition, in order to fix them upon the mind. Teach them to your younger friends, in order to establish your own knowledge while you communicate it to them. The animal powers of your tongue and of your ear, as well as your intellectual faculties, will all join together to help the memory. Hermetus studied hard in a remote corner of the land, and in solitude, yet he became a very learned man. He seldom was so happy as to enjoy suitable society at home, and therefore he talked over to the fields and the woods in the evening what he had been reading in the day. . . .

ISAAC WATTS (1741)

■ An example of grouping ideas in significant ways

Imagine that you have to learn in detail the psychology of Abraham Maslow and that you are studying the graphic aid

in *The Third Force: The Psychology of Abraham Maslow**
reprinted here. To remember the sixteen "growth needs,"
you should look for a basis of clustering or grouping the
terms which is consistent with Maslow's psychology. You
should avoid grouping on insignificant bases such as alpha-
betizing, common suffixes, or forming a sentence from
words that begin with the first letter of each of the growth
needs.

How might you cluster or group the growth needs then?
Realizing that, according to Maslow's theories, growth
needs are

1. nonhierarchical (that is, have no particular order of
   precedence)
2. derived from Maslow's study of individuals who seem
   to have achieved "self-actualization"

you could group the growth needs in fours according to your
own conception of related needs or characteristics and then
think of someone you know who seems to exemplify each of
the four groups.

To recall the growth needs, you would then simply recall
the four individuals you know who exemplify the characteristics; by association, you would remember the groups of
related terms (needs/characteristics) that you have identified
with the four individuals. By studying this way, you would
not only remember the sixteen growth needs but also better
understand the psychological theory of Abraham Maslow.

(1)	(2)	(3)	(4)
Truth	Aliveness	Necessity	Completion
Goodness	Individuality	Justice	Simplicity
Beauty	Richness	Order	Effortlessness
Perfection	Playfulness	Self-sufficiency	Meaningfulness

Exemplified by

1) _____ 2) _____ 3) _____ 4) _____

---

*Frank Goble, *The Third Force: The Psychology of Abraham Maslow*,
p. 52. Copyright © 1970 by Thomas Jefferson Research Center. Reprinted by permission of Viking-Penguin, a division of Penguin Books
USA, Inc

Abraham Maslow's Hierarchy of Needs

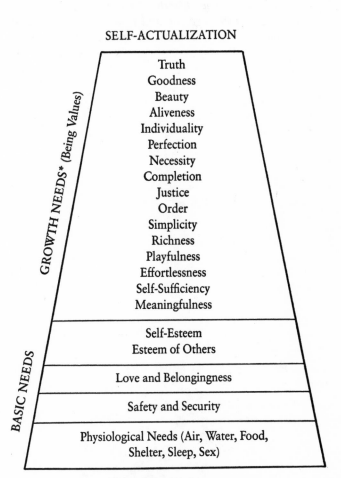

The External Environment
Preconditions for Need Satisfaction:
Freedom, Justice, Orderliness,
Challenge (Stimulation)

---

*Growth needs are all of equal importance (not hierarchical).

*W*hatsoever you would trust to your memory let it be disposed in a proper method, connected well together, and referred to distinct and particular heads or classes both general and particular.

ISAAC WATTS (1741)

■ Taking Examinations

■ Essay examinations

1. Prepare to begin: Take several slow, deep breaths through your nose. Check the time and ask whether it will be announced at all during the exam.
2. Underline key words in the directions and questions to focus your thinking, help you keep calm, and prevent you from trying to write before you are settled and organized.
3. Read through all of the questions; jot down a few words that come to mind about each question you plan to answer (if there is a choice).

> Read through all of the questions; jot down a few words that come to mind about each question you plan to answer.

4. Budget your time.
   a) Consider the number of points given for each question, if this information is stated.
   b) Decide how much time you should allot for each answer.
   c) Allow time for a rough outline before writing each answer and for proofreading after completing the exam.

5. As a rule, answer the easiest question (or second easiest) first, to increase your confidence and give you more time to recall answers for the harder questions.

6. Jot down a rough outline from which to write your answer to each question.

   a) In a column, write key words and phrases related to points that you remember from lectures and from your reading and thinking for the course.

   b) Then think *beyond* these first ideas to new ideas that occur to you in response to the question; these ideas may be based upon your own experiences and interests as well as the lectures and readings for the course.

   c) Number your points in the most appropriate order.

   d) If you run out of time in answering the question, copy points from your outline to complete your answer briefly.

7. Take care to answer precisely the question asked.

   a) Notice especially the limitation stressed by the verb (list, analyze, compare).

   b) Form the first sentence by turning the question into a statement or by writing a thesis sentence that you will support with specific examples or evidence.

   c) Include a time frame, indicating, for example, whether a historical movement extended over decades or centuries.

   d) When in doubt, qualify your answers by using approximate times or dates and by including qualifying words (for example, "some" or "most," "usually" or "occasionally") in your statements.

   e) Underline the key phrases in your answer, so that the hurried exam reader will not miss a single one of them.

   8) Begin a new paragraph for each point on your outline.

9. Support your main points with carefully chosen evidence or examples.

10. Abbreviate long names or terms that you will need to repeat frequently and include a code at the top of the

Support your main points with carefully chosen evidence or examples.

page on which you first use the abbreviation (for example, T = Tchaikovsky; R = Revolution).

11. Write clearly, concisely, and legibly. (If you prefer to type, inquire in advance about the possibility of typing your exam.)

12. Leave a space after each paragraph to allow for possible additions when you proofread; or write your answers only on the front side of each page so that you can insert additions on the back of the preceding page.

13. Proofread your answer.

14. Take care to use returned tests to determine how to study for and take tests more successfully.

■ Sample essay question

If you were given an examination on the material in this book, an appropriate question might be this one:

What advice would you give a friend who asks you for help with a serious problem—his tendency to panic at exam time?

On a separate piece of paper, follow steps 6 through 13 for taking essay examinations; then compare what you have written with the sample essay illustrated here in longhand.

Question rephrased in opening statement.

If a friend asked me for advice about his problem of panicking at exam time, this is what I would tell him.

Question interpreted broadly.

Consider yourself _preparing for exams from the first day of class_. Learn each chunk of new material as you encounter it; for example, learn lecture notes within 24 hours after every class. Preview all nonfiction material recommended and read it selectively; delay taking notes about the content (noting instead pages and parts-of-pages to which you may return for notetaking), but note immediately your own ideas about the material. Preview required textbook chapters, and prepare a one-page outline of each chapter as you read it

Space left between paragraphs.

Plan a special review several days before the exam. Begin by building a table of contents for your class notes Plan your study time by estimating how much time you'll need to review one chunk and multiplying by the number of chunks you have.

Write on your calendar when you should study each chunk, counting back from the date the exam is scheduled. Study actively; for example, create graphic aids and formulate answers to anticipated exam questions as you study. Two nights (at least) before the exam, exchange anticipated questions with a friend and outline your answers to unfamiliar questions; in this way you'll be having almost a dress rehearsal of the exam. The night before the exam, get enough sleep so that you will feel as alert and able to cope as possible.

Main points underlined.

<u>Take precautions in taking the exam.</u> Underline key words in the directions and in the questions to calm your nerves and keep you from starting to write before you're ready. Budget your time, allowing first for a rough outline of your answer and last for proofreading. Skip lines after each paragraph to allow space for inserting any new ideas you think of during proofreading.

<u>Take advantage of professional counseling</u> or University Counseling Service workshops to overcome test anxiety. For this to be most effective, do it at least two months before your exams.

Briefly then, overcoming panic at exam time is likely to require regular study from the very beginning of the course, special preparation several days in advance of the exam, precautions while taking the exam, and perhaps - for best results - the help of a counseling psychologist.

Main points summarized—an aspect of this essay that goes beyond the recommendations given in this booklet. See #6b on page 88.

■ Objective examinations

The brief suggestions below are for taking verbal aptitude tests. For more extensive suggestions for taking objective tests, see *How to Take Tests*, by Jason Millman and Walter Pauk (New York: McGraw-Hill, 1969). For help in taking objective examinations in the health sciences, see *Test-Taking Skills: A Programmed Text for Medicine and Health Sciences*, by Randolph Sarnacke (Baltimore: University Park Press, 1981), or *Test-Taking Skills in Dentistry*, by Randolph E. Sarnacki (Philadelphia: Lea and Ferbinger, 1982).

Word opposites

1. Note that you are searching for word *opposites*, or antonyms, not synonyms. Because it is usually quicker and easier to think of synonyms, think of the given word as changed to its opposite—by adding "not" to a positive word or by cutting the "un-" or "in-" negative prefix from a negative word. Then search among the multiple choices for a word that means the same as the word(s) now in your mind. For example, change "laborious" to "not laborious," and you will recognize immediately that "easy" is the best answer.
2. If the given word is only slightly familiar to you, but at least you know whether it has a "good" or "bad" connotation, it is probably worth the time to try to answer the question.
3. However, (a) if the given word is totally unfamiliar to you, (b) if you cannot guess even its connotation by examining its root or thinking of words similar in form or sound to it, and (c) if you can't eliminate even one multiple choice as definitely wrong, move on to the next question rather than waste time trying to think of the answer.

Try out the above suggestions on these examples from the Graduate Record Examination Information Bulletin (Princeton, N.J.: Educational Testing Service), 1988–1989. Reprinted by permission.

REFUTABLE: (A) understandable (B) unavoidable (C) indispensable (D) inexpressible (E) indisputable

EXODUS: (A) search (B) retraction (C) influx (D) application (E) meeting

Analogies

1. Before reading any of the multiple choices, decide at least two ways in which the key words are related. For example, "torch: liberty": (1) a torch is a symbol of liberty, and (2) a torch is held by the Statue of Liberty.
2. Remember that analogous relationships are usually one of the following kinds:
   a) Part to whole ("spring: watch")
   b) Degree ("hard: formidable")
   c) Cause and effect ("puncture: blowout")
   d) Chronology ("tadpole: frog")
   e) Symbol to symbolized ("torch: liberty")
3. In reading the multiple choices, first consider choices for only *one* of the two words in the given analogy; eliminate several of the multiple choices that do not fit your anticipated answer, then consider the second half of the analogy in the choices remaining.

Try out the above suggestions on these examples from the Graduate Record Examination Information Bulletin (Princeton, N.J.: Educational Testing Service), 1988–1989. Reprinted by permission.

EPILOGUE: NOVEL:: (A) lyric: poem (B) violin: sonata (C) title: sermon (D) song: cycle (E) coda: symphony

RECOMMEND: LAUD:: (A) suggest: deduce (B) assume: instigate (C) calculate: arrange (D) sanction: foster (E) believe: persuade

Sentence completions

1. Read the whole sentence, with blanks, and decide which blank (if there are two) seems easiest to fill.
2. Think about the kind of word that might fit the blank that seems easiest to fill.

3. Read the multiple choices for the one blank only and choose two possible answers from the choices.
4. Reread the whole sentence, substituting multiple choices *only* for the two pairs of choices that you have decided are possibly correct.

Reading comprehension

1. Preview the paragraph(s) by reading:
   a) the first sentence of the first paragraph
   b) the last paragraph
   c) the first and last sentences of any other paragraphs.
2. Read the first two questions *without* reading the multiple choices.
3. Read the whole selection with these questions in mind.
4. Read the multiple choices for the first two questions and answer the questions.
5. Use appropriate reading approaches to answer the other questions, for example scan for details, carefully read a sentence or paragraph in which a metaphor must be explained.
6. To answer questions about inferences or conclusions, select two or three possibilities from the multiple choices. Test each possibility by rereading the paragraph with one inference in mind. When or if a phrase or sentence seems to contradict that inference, stop reading the paragraph and start again with another inference in mind.

Note: In taking multiple-choice tests, keep in mind that statistics show that if you can identify at least one of the multiple choices as wrong, you're fairly safe in guessing the answer; if you can identify at least two of the choices as wrong, you're wise to guess the answer.

In order to discover the value of these procedures and in order to make the procedures habitual, apply them on numerous examples of each type of question in a reputable book of sample multiple-choice examinations.

You can obtain the current edition of the Graduate Record Examination Information Bulletin from:

Graduate Record Examinations
Educational Testing Service
Box 6000
Princeton, NJ 08541-6000

■ Improving Concentration, Motivation, and Willpower

Concentration, motivation, and willpower—attitudes that are essential for the most effective and efficient reading and study—can usually be improved in four basic ways:

1. Study actively and efficiently, using methods like those described in this book; by doing so, you can shorten the time in which you must concentrate, motivate yourself, and use your willpower.
   a) Organize your work and budget your time.
   b) Increase your background in the subject matter, and so increase your interest in it.
   c) Preview before reading expository material, then chunk the material; chew and swallow one chunk before biting off another.
   d) If you tend to procrastinate before or after previewing, start reading at the part of the book or article that you find most interesting.
   e) In starting on a research paper, delay taking notes on what a book says, but note your own ideas and questions about it immediately; confirm your plans for the paper with your professor or supervisor before proceeding further.
2. Provide for favorable study conditions, like these:
   a) times of day when you feel alert enough to concentrate;

b) adequate light and ventilation;
c) freedom from distractions (for example, noise: if you cannot prevent or move away from distracting noise, set up a closer nondistracting sound, like music without words or a fan);
d) a seat in which you can be comfortable but also alert;

e) regular exercise, sufficient sleep, and at least three nourishing (but not heavy) meals a day;
f) recently prescribed glasses, if you need them for reading;
g) freedom from substances that interfere with concentration, such as caffeine, and many other drugs;
h) occasional study with a carefully chosen group, with fixed times for starting and ending.
3. Give attention to possible psychological causes of inadequate concentration, motivation, or willpower.
   a) Talk with a psychologist at a university counseling service or with a psychiatrist at a university mental health service or in private practice.
   b) Read books that can give you insight into your attitudes and behavior.
4. Try to clarify your immediate and long-term goals.
   a) Discuss your goals with an academic advisor, psy-

chologists at a counseling service, and personnel at a career planning and placement service.

b) Read both fiction and nonfiction that relates to the career you have been considering.

c) Seek actual experience in the field you have been considering and/or talk at length with individuals who seem to be successful in the field.

Now in order to gain a greater facility of attention we may observe these rules:

1. 'Get a good liking to the study or knowledge you would pursue.' We may observe that there is not much difficulty in confining the mind to contemplate what we have a great desire to know. . . .

2. 'Do not choose your constant place of study by the finery of the prospects, or the most various and entertaining scenes of sensible things.' Too much light, or a variety of objects which strike the eye or the ear, especially while they are ever in motion or often changing, have a natural and powerful tendency to steal away the mind too often from its steady pursuit of any subject which we contemplate. . . .

ISAAC WATTS (1741)

As you try just a few of the recommendations, you are likely to experience one small success after another. Each success will increase your confidence and relieve your anxiety—and so improve your concentration, motivation, and willpower.

If you follow the recommendations in this guide and find that you don't progress as much or as rapidly as you had anticipated, arrange for an interview about your reading, writing, and study needs at a university reading/writing improvement service or learning center.

■ Keeping Up in Your Profession: Lifelong Learning

You have graduated from college and perhaps from graduate or professional school, and you are beginning to work in your new job or profession. You know that keeping up with current knowledge in your field and related disciplines is a professional responsibility and that it not only makes you better at what you do, it makes you more interested in it and enthusiastic about it. But how can you work in a demanding profession, keep up with current knowledge in and beyond your immediate areas of responsibility, and also lead a reasonably balanced life? Keeping up is difficult to manage, but it will be easier and take less time if you go about it in an organized way.

When you are working in your field, you will necessarily be keeping up with many of the aspects related to your immediate responsibilities. To keep up more broadly and efficiently, you will need to use strategies like these, adapting them to your particular profession and style:

1. Through universities, libraries and bookstores, professional organizations, and publishers in your field, find authorities and consult them frequently.
   a) Universities, libraries and bookstores:
      1) Browse in university and specialized bookstores that stock books for courses in your field and closely related fields. In each book that looks useful, scan the index for topics of particular interest to you, read the table of contents and pre-

view chapters of immediate interest. This can help you "keep up" as well as decide what to buy.

2) Examine the syllabi of courses in your field or related fields and choose one or more courses to take or audit.

3) With the help of a reference librarian, make a computerized search for summaries of articles on a subject of your professional interest. Reading the summaries can give you a good overview of information and materials available on the subject and help you decide confidently which materials to locate and read more fully.

4) Examine a "current awareness" publication regularly; for example, *Current Contents* (published by the Institute for Scientific Information, Philadelphia, Pa.) reprints the tables of contents of current journals in various fields—*Current Contents for Social and Behavioral Sciences, . . . Life Sciences, . . . Arts and Humanities, . . . Engineering, Technology and Applied Science, and . . . Physical, Chemical and Earth Sciences.*

5) Clip or photocopy reviews of books that you might want to buy.

b) Professional organizations:

1) Join one or more professional organizations, at least for a year's trial. Some organizations have

reduced rates for the first year or for student members.

2) Subscribe to at least one journal published by each organization that you join; attend some of the organizations' seminars, conferences, or conventions; and buy some books and tapes that they make available.

3) If you cannot attend a conference you are interested in, ask the sponsors for a program and occasionally write to speakers requesting copies of their presentation or any materials distributed.

4) Submit articles of your own to journals of the organizations or prepare presentations for their conferences.

c) Publishers:

1) Browse through the catalogs of publishing companies in your field, note books for possible ordering, and request that your name be added to the publishers' mailing lists.

2) Save time and avoid errors in purchasing books by browsing in the publishers' exhibits that are part of many professional conventions and placing orders there for books you have examined.

3) Buy a current dictionary or handbook for your field.

2. Prepare to keep up with your reading by previewing and selecting.

a) When you add a book or journal to your library, or borrow one from a friend in your field or from a library, take a few minutes to prepare to read it. In the table of contents, if the book is your own, make a short line or question mark next to each chapter or article that you think you want to read soon. If you have borrowed the book, photocopy the title page, copyright notice, and table of contents so that you can mark them freely and save them for future reference.

b) As soon as possible, preview sections, chapters, or articles of immediate interest to get a sense of their scope and quality and to satisfy your curiosity temporarily. Make an X by any articles or chapters that you think are not worth reading further.

c) If you want to remember what you previewed, tell yourself or a companion about it from memory, before moving on.

> Prepare to keep up with your reading by previewing and selecting.

d) When you expect to travel or have some other appropriate time for reading professional material, take the books or journals that you have previewed and selected.

3. Make notes appropriate for your purposes.

a) When you read, make notes according to the sections of this book on "Saving Time in Taking Notes" and "Critical and Creative Reading."

b) Write the notes in any of several places, according to how or where you want to store your notes: at the top of the first page of the article or chapter, on the flyleaf, on index cards, or on 8½ × 11 paper. Two of the advantages of making most of your notes on separate cards or pages, rather than in the books or journals themselves, are that the books will be more readable without distracting marks (for you and others who read or reread them in the future) and you will still have the notes if you give away or lend or lose the book.

c) Note a reminder of your overall judgment of each chapter or article by appropriate marks in the margins of the table of contents; for example, by checks: $\checkmark$, $\checkmark-$, or $\checkmark+$. Writing symbols in the table of contents can be helpful to you immediately and at many points in your professional future, up to the day when you decide to give away some of the hundreds or thousands of books and journals which you have accumulated through the years. All you will need to do is look for a √ + on the cover or the table of contents to decide whether you should keep the material.

d) In the margins of the table of contents, next to the titles of the portions you have read, write the pages and parts-of-pages you found especially valuable.

e) Photocopy pages that you must keep readily accessible. Also photocopy the title page, copyright notice, and table of contents, or note complete bibliographical information directly on the first or last page of each copy; you will need this information later if you want to cite the material or write for permission to use it. (See the appendix of this book for information about "Copyright Law: An Increasing Concern to Students and Professionals.") Determine the key word or subject under which you should file the pages, and file them either temporarily in an alphabetized accordian file or permanently in indexed file folders or the like.

4. If you have accumulated quantities of books and journals but given them little more than a glance, bring yourself to read them by previewing, chunking, and selecting.

a) Preview and chunk: Look over all the books, group them by the subjects of concern to you, and subgroup them alphabetically by author.

> Begin reading at the part
> that appeals to you most.

b) Preview and select: Preview a few books that particularly appeal to you, and select one of these to start reading as thoroughly as necessary. Begin reading at the part that appeals to you most, thus lessening any tendency you may have to procrastination. Having started so well, you might feel inspired to move on to the next most appealing part,

or to go back and read from page one—or to move
on to a different book.

c) When you encounter a part that you especially
want to remember, tell yourself or a companion
about it from memory.

d) Keep a looseleaf memo book in your pocket or
pocketbook, one with pages the same size as the index cards you use regularly, so that you can note
new ideas, information, or references immediately,
and can file the notes easily.

5. File your notes and photocopies systematically, for
ready retrieval. Browse in a well-stocked stationery or
office-supply store and buy and use various kinds of
aids to filing, like these:

a) for short-term storage, when you are in a hurry,
large accordion notebooks or envelopes, with alphabetic tabs, and file boxes with index cards and
dividers;

b) for long-term storage, when you have time to file
more carefully, containers of various types and sizes
with self-stick labels—shelves, file drawers and
cabinets, three-ring notebooks with dividers that
have pockets;

c) for longest-term storage, when you want the materials to remain in good condition for as long as
possible, acid-free containers, which are available
through companies that sell archival material (mu-
seum or library personnel can refer you to these
companies).

6. Exchange information and ideas with colleagues.

a) Participate in continuing education that may be
provided in your workplace.

b) Initiate continuing education. For example, organize a discussion group for interested members of
your profession and related fields.

c) Meet colleagues for lunch and informal exchange
of information and ideas—including ideas about
keeping up in your field or profession.

7. If and when you decide to change fields, cut back to
part-time, or retire, enjoy additional fruits of lifelong
learning.

a) Give away or sell books and journals that you no longer need and that others might find helpful.

1) If you haven't marked all over your books, they will be more readable by others, so that you can sell them or trade them, give them to friends, or contribute them (with an income tax deduction) to professional libraries. Some institutions have sibling institutions, often ones in developing countries, for which gifts of books are welcome. An office of planned giving or international programs in the benefactor institution may take care of shipping the books.

2) If you decide to give away large numbers of books and journals, employ a librarian to list and assess them. Copies of such an assessment can give you an accurate record of your gift's value for income tax deductions; they can make your gift more useful to the institution to which you give them, and they can remind you of which books and journals you gave away, if you start looking for one in its former place in your library.

3) If you audit courses, join reading groups, or read extensively on your own, you may want to continue using methods that have helped you learn more in less time. Or you may simply want to enjoy reading without concern for how much

you remember. More and more you may agree
with Sir Francis Bacon in his essay. "Of Studies":
"Some books are to be tasted, others to be
swallowed, and some few to be chewed and
digested."

■ Bibliography

The following books are recommended as additional sources of ideas or encouragement for improving reading, writing, and study. See also the bibliographies in the sections on "Reading Fiction and Poetry . . ." and on "Improving Writing."

Barnet Sylvan. *A Short Guide to Writing about Art.* 3rd ed. Glenview, Ill.: Scott Foresman, 1988.

Brengelman, Fred. *Understanding Words: Systematic Spelling and Vocabulary Building.* Dubuque, Iowa: Kendall/Hunt, 1980.

Burns, David D. *Feeling Good: The New Mood Therapy.* New York: New American Library, 1981.

Gibaldi, Joseph, and Walter S. Achtert, eds. *MLA Handbook for Writers of Research Papers, Theses and Dissertations.* 3rd ed. New York: Modern Language Association, 1988.

Lakein, Alan. *How to Get Control of Your Time and Your Life.* New York: New American Library, 1974.

Mann, Thomas. *A Guide to Library Research Methods.* New York: Oxford University Press, 1987.

Millman, Jason, and Walter Pauk. *How to Take Tests.* New York: McGraw-Hill, 1969.

Pauk, Walter. *How to Study in College.* 4th ed. Boston: Houghton Mifflin, 1989.

Publication Manual of the American Psychological Association. Washington, D.C.: American Psychological Association, 1983.

Ronstadt, Ronald. *The Art of Case Analysis: A Guide to the Diagnosis of Business Situations.* 2nd ed. Dover, Mass.: Lord, 1980.

■ Appendix

■ Copyright Law: An Increasing Concern to Students and Professionals

The main purpose of copyright laws has been to protect the rights of authors and artists and their publishers, for the ultimate benefit of the public. The first copyright law in the United States, which was enacted by Congress in 1790, was designed to protect publishers' rights to copy material. Over the years, as copyright law has changed, its emphasis has shifted to protecting authors' and artists' rights to control copying of their intellectual works.

The doctrine of Fair Use, which originated in the 1840s, limits the rights of authors, artists, and publishers, by allowing certain kinds of copying which are not considered infringements of the law. The current interpretation of Fair Use, and a few other provisions of the most recent copyright law (1976), are explained briefly in the excerpts below, from Harry G. Henn's *Copyright Law: A Practitioners' Guide*, 2nd ed. (Practising Law Institute, 1988).

Caution regarding unauthorized copying or copyright infringement will become increasingly important, because in March 1989 the United States joined, at last, the Bern Union, the Union Internationale pour la Protection des Oeuvres Littéraires et Artistiques. This is a hundred-year-old international union of over sixty countries, with headquarters in Bern, Switzerland. Each country belonging to the Union grants citizens of other member countries the same copyright privileges as its own citizens. Although the United States has not acceded to all the provisions of the Bern convention, copyright law will be increasingly significant, in view of the added protection afforded to authors and publishers when a country becomes a signatory to the Bern convention.

For more information about current copyright law in the United States, write or call the Copyright Office in the Library of Congress, to request its free packet of informational materials (which, like all U.S. Government materials, are not copyrighted). The address of the Copyright Office is 101 Independence Avenue, SE, Washington DC 20540; telephone 202-479-0700. If you need specific legal advice, especially about copying material created by citizens of countries other than your own, consult an attorney.

When in doubt about using any copyrighted material, always write to the publisher, at least three months in advance of when you need to use the material, for permission to copy it. Be sure to describe or list the pages you want to copy, your intended audience, and your purposes. The permissions editor will tell you whether or not you can have permission to copy the material and the conditions involved, in particular the form of the acknowledgment that will be necessary and the fee, if any.

Excerpts from *Copyright Law: A Practitioner's Guide*, **2nd ed. by Harry G. Henn. New York: Practising Law Institute, 1988, supp. 1989.**

18. FAIR USE

A. In General

The 1976 Act provided no definitions of fair use [one of the exceptions to the copyright law], but suggests criteria. Whether a use is fair depends upon:

1. The "purpose" of the use; and
2. At least four "factors."

B. Purposes

Use can be "fair" for "purposes" "such as" criticism, comment, news reporting, teaching (including multiple copies for classroom use), scholarship, or research (pp. 182–183).

C. Factors

In determining whether the use "in any particular case" is a fair use, the "factors" to be considered shall "include" (p. 184):

1. The "purpose" and "character" of the use, including whether such use is of a "commercial nature" or is "for nonprofit educational purposes";
2. The "nature" of the copyrighted work;
3. The "amount and substantiality of the portion used" in relation to the copyrighted work as a whole; and
4. The effect of the use upon the "potential market for or value of" the copyrighted work. (p. 185)

This fourth factor, "the effect of the use upon the potential market for or value of the copyrighted work," "is undoubtedly the single most important element of fair use."

• • •

1. Classroom Copying of Books and Periodicals

The guidelines for classroom copying in not-for-profit educational institutions with respect to books and periodicals were prepared by representatives of the Ad Hoc Committee of Educational Institutions and Organizations on Copyright Law Revision, the Authors League of America, Inc., and the Association of American Publishers, Inc. Although not binding, the guidelines significantly influence courts, and have the practical impact of statutory provisions.

a) Single Copies

A teacher may reproduce a *single* copy, subject to "prohibitions," for research or teaching purposes, of:

1) A chapter from a book;
2) An article from a periodical or newspaper;
3) A short story, short essay, or short poem, whether or not from a collective work;
4) A chart, graph, diagram, drawing, cartoon, or picture from a book, periodical, or newspaper. (p. 189)

b) Multiple Copies

A teacher may make *multiple* copies for classroom use if the copying meets certain tests for brevity, spontaneity, and cumulative effect. Each copy must also include a notice of copyright. (p. 190)

c) Prohibitions

Prohibitions applicable to both single and multiple copying are:

1) The copies may not be used for anthologies, compilations, or collective works;
2) "Consumable" materials, such as workbooks, tests, and answer sheets, may not be copied;
3) Copying may not be used to substitute for purchasing, be "directed by higher authority," or be repeated "with respect to the same item by the same teacher from term to term";
4) The student may not be charged more than the actual costs of the photocopying. (p. 191)

• • •

19. REPRODUCTION AND DISTRIBUTION BY LIBRARIES AND ARCHIVES

B. Conditions

The rights of reproduction and distribution of a library or archives, or any of its employees acting within the scope of their employment, are limited to "no more than one copy or phonorecord of a work" and are subject to three specified overall conditions: (p. 202)

1. The making must be "without any purpose of direct or indirect commercial advantage";
2. The collections of the library or archives must be open to the public or available not only to affiliated researchers but also to other persons "doing research in a specialized field"; and
3. The reproduction or distribution must include a "notice of copyright " (p 203)

2. Liability of User of Reproducing Equipment or Requester of Copies or Phonorecords

Liability for copyright infringement of a person who uses the reproducing equipment in a library or archive or who requests copies or phonorecords of articles or other contributions to a copyrighted collection or periodical issue or of a small part of any other copyrighted work for any such act, or for any later use of such copy or phonorecord, if it exceeds fair use, is not excused by the libraries-and-archives provisions. (p. 212)

• • •

G. Future Prospects

There are growing disputes between publishers and authors, on the one hand, and librarians and educators, on the other.

A private Copyright Clearance Center (CCC) was established in 1977 to collect fees from photocopiers and to divide the proceeds among copyright owners. In 1984, the Center began to issue blanket licenses under a contract fee based on statistical samples for periodicals and journals ("Annual Authorization Service"). As a result, increased numbers of corporations have subscribed. The Center has been denied tax-exempt status. (pp. 214–215)